Adventures in Healing

CLOSE ENCOUNTERS
WITH JOHN OF GOD AND THE
SPIRIT BROTHERS OF BRAZIL

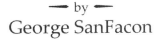

— by —

George SanFacon

1st printing...January 2012
2nd printing...June 2012

Layout and design by:
hEDWERXdESIGN
2807 N Kedzie Avenue, 3rd Floor
Chicago, IL 60618
www.hedwerxdesign.com
email: asf@hedwerxdesign.com
phone: 773-206-4215

Published by:
Charing Cross Press
P.O. Box 6052
Ann Arbor, MI 48106-6052
email: HLRideas@umich.edu
phone: 734-971-3455

Books can be ordered from Charing Cross Press at a cost of $13 ($10 for book plus $3 mailing charge if required), or online at www.Amazon.com.

Printed in United States of America.

ISBN: 978-0-9826320-4-8

Table of Contents

Dedication

to Amara Grace and Ashton Michael…
with love, Grandpa George

A Word from the Author

This writing is centered around a month-long visit at John of God's spiritual healing center and sanctuary—the Casa de Dom Ignacio or just "the Casa"— in Brazil during January 2011. While I journeyed there with close friends and acquaintances, I recount here only my own, direct personal experience, starting prior to the actual trip and ending several months afterward. What follows is not so much a travelogue or road journal, but a summary of the most significant experiences, healings, and insights I had at the Casa and afterward. While these occurred within the context of what is called "Spiritism," they have universal application regardless of the reader's faith or denomination.

The writing was done primarily to support my own inner process, helping me to better understand and integrate my experience there. After sharing an early draft with family and friends, it seemed that the material could possibly benefit others, too. So it is now in your hands.

But be forewarned: the material can be challenging. Why? In part, because it reveals a lot about the deeper landscape of my interior life, which some folks will find strange or difficult to comprehend. Even more so, however, is the phantasmagorical nature of the John of God phenomenon, where the normal boundary lines of experience—separating the real from the imaginal, the actual from the possible, the believable from the unbelievable—can vanish. I have, therefore, tried to be careful in both processing and describing my experience, placing the emphasis on *reporting* rather than on *interpreting*. While I certainly believe that "something has been going on," I do not claim to know what it is. For those looking to explain the phenomena described herein, I can only suggest the following possibilities: spirit-beings, extraterrestrials, universal field effects, parallel realities, cosmic wormholes, archetypal patterns in the psyche, hallucinations, psychotic breakdown, neurological disorder, and/or some combination thereof. Take your pick.

Kind thoughts come ...

George

Brooklyn, Michigan
August 2011

GETTING READY

Deciding to Go (October 2010)

"If you could ask for and receive *any* healings that you wanted, what would you ask for? ... Would the healings be physical, psychological, mental, or spiritual? ... Would they be just for you, or would they be for others, too?" These were the questions I pondered after spontaneously agreeing to accompany my dear friend Kris on a journey to see the world-renowned, mediumistic healer, known as "John of God," in Abadiania, Brazil. Besides deciding on specific goals for healing, there was also the issue of justifying a 9,000 mile round trip made possible by the use of nonrenewable fossil fuels. Not an easy thing to do for a so-called environmentalist.

Ultimately, the two issues—deciding upon a healing request and justifying the trip—came together. The trip and healing had to serve the larger good. Eventually, I committed to the journey as "a pilgrimage in service to all beings." First, I would help make it feasible for Kris to travel there in search of a cure for her muscular dystrophy. Second, I would serve as an ambassador and courier carrying long-distance healing requests on behalf of family and friends (more on these healing requests later). Third, I would seek my own healing to "end the war" against what is, open my heart, and renew myself to better serve my family and the world in the years ahead. I was told by our group leader and guide, Barbara, that once you make the decision to go and set your intention, John of God and the healing Entities immediately begin working with you.

Getting Ready (November and December)

For the next few weeks, I found myself spontaneously telling people about the upcoming trip—family, friends, fellow environmental activists, folks at the local coffee shop, even doctors and nurses who administered the recommended vaccines (Tetanus, Typhoid, Yellow Fever, Hepatitis A, and Hepatitis B). I encouraged each of them to check out "John of God" on the Internet, and let me know if they wanted me to carry a healing request on their behalf. This required that I take along and submit a photo of the individual dressed in white, with their full legal name, nickname, date of birth, address, and requested healings written on the back. Eventually, 30 people took me up on the offer.

I prepared for the journey in other ways, too. Starting in November, I reinstituted my meditation practice. I sat almost daily for an hour or so anytime between 5 and 8 am, simultaneously with the Current at the Casa (more about the Current later). I also changed my sitting posture, as recommended by Barbara. She suggested that we not cross our legs or arms, thereby remaining "open" physically and energetically. She also recommended that we spend time focused on: (1) our intentions and request for healing, (2) being open to receive what healing is available, and (3) sending healing intentions and energy out into the world for others. I incorporated all of these suggestions, and found it surprisingly easy to do the early morning sittings. Even though I have been meditating on and off for 20 years, there has typically been some resistance to it. It usually shows up in my wanting to skip the meditation and sleep in longer, or cut it sort to begin engaging on my "to do" list for the day. Remarkably, throughout this period, I had no such resistance and found the sittings to be easy, expansive, and exhilarating.

I also checked out the John of God's website (www.friendsofthecasa.org), which has video footage of John of God doing physical surgeries on people without anesthesia or antibiotics, as well as a *Casa Guide* for English-speaking people. I read several books related to the John of God phenomenon, his healing center in Abadiania, people's experience there, and the Spiritist movement in general. The best and most helpful of those were *The Spirits' Book* by Alan Kardec (written in the 1850s), *The Book of Miracles* by Josie RavenWing, and *Spiritual Alliances* by Emma Bragden. The first provides a general overview and orientation on Spiritist doctrine, while the other two provide fascinating explanations and accounts of the system and experience at John of God's spiritual center.

Besides the meditation and research, I also took three *crystal baths* (more about crystal baths later). This was made possible by friends, Anna Marie and Jack, who had brought a device back with them from the Casa the previous year. The baths were recommended before the trip because they reputedly help to clear and fine tune major energy centers of the body (called "chakras"), thereby expediting the healing process at the Casa.

Other preparations included my getting a visa, procuring Brazilian currency ($1,000 U.S. equivalent through a local travel agency), and purchasing miscellaneous items. These included white clothes for wearing at the Casa (white enables the healing Entities to better see and "read" the auric body), sunscreen, insect repellant, first-aid supplies, some dried fruits and nuts, and a travel alarm clock. Packing was not a problem, as I was allowed two checked bags (each weighing up to 70 pounds and measuring up to 62 inches, including length, width and height) and two carry-ons (my trusty backpack and a laptop computer). I also needed to consider what reading materials to take. Eventually, I decided to only take books related to my spiritual practice and healing: *Genuine Happiness* by B. Allan Wallace, *The Most Direct Means to Eternal Bliss* by Michal Langford, *Wake Up to Your Life* by Ken McLeod, and *The Fine Arts of Relaxation, Concentration and Meditation* by Joel and Michelle Levey.

Synchronicities

Several synchronicities occurred during this time. And as synchronicities go, they somehow happened without conscious effort on my part and mysteriously facilitated the experience that was unfolding.

> *Accessing a Crystal Bed.* The local availability of a crystal bed was unusual. In Michigan, there are only a few of them available to the public. And the one I had access to was portable, so that Kris and I were each able to have sessions at her place.

> *Finding Time to Do Research.* After each of my first two crystal baths I was bedridden for two days, completely overcome with some kind of across-the-board physical fatigue. Fortunately, I had no previous commitments for those days, and I remained strangely clear and mentally alert. I was, therefore, able to take full advantage of the "down time" by reading the related books I had purchased. These had conveniently arrived a few days earlier and, strangely, were the only reading materials that evoked any interest for me. Not only did I read them, I easily retained a remarkable amount of the information.

> *Getting Healing Requests from Others.* Connecting with family and friends about the opportunity for their own healing was greatly facilitated by the Christmas holidays. I simply carried my cell phone (which has a camera) and a white bathrobe with me during holiday visits. This made it an easy matter to get

photos of people in white, which I would then email to Kris who printed them out for the trip.

Receiving Injunctions for Getting Started. I spontaneously began reading a book that my friend Bernie had referred to on several occasions, *Joy's Way* by Brugh Joy. Among other things, the book admonishes us to: (1) give up comparisons, (2) make no judgments, and (3) let go of the need to understand. The first two of these injunctions laid important groundwork for my healing. I could readily sense how comparison and judgment were contributing to the heaviness I felt around my heart. The third injunction helped prepare me to "receive" the remarkable experience ahead.

Having John of God "Legitimized" on the Oprah Show. Lastly, the undertaking had raised some serious concerns on the part of a few of my family members. But shortly after I announced my plans, Oprah dedicated an entire show to the John of God phenomenon and his healing center in Abadiania. This not only relieved folks, but also influenced them in deciding to take me up on my offer to carry healing requests on their behalf.

Opening for the Experience

The material I read on *Spiritism* and about John of God was challenging for me. According to Spiritist doctrine, we are spirits created by God (or the Source) and have eternal life. As spirits, we freely and consciously choose to incarnate as humans into this world to do work that furthers our development and evolution. By incarnating again and again over many lifetimes and doing our work, we purify ourselves and move ever closer to *perfection*. This so-called "perfection" is a spirit that is wise, compassionate, and happy, and that willingly contributes to the transformation of others in their own evolution.

John of God, or Joao (pronounced "ja-ow" as in "ouch"), has had a lifelong experience—beginning when he was nine years old—of being an unconscious channel, or medium, for higher-level spirits that come into this world and heal. His full Brazilian birth name is Joao Teixeira de Faria, and he is referred to as "John of God" by admirers. But when he is incorporated as a medium and there is a spirit or other energy that is coming through him, that energy is referred to as "the Entity." There are over 30 distinct entities that live on the spiritual plane and use Joao as a channel, most of them famous saints and healers, including King Solomon, St. Ignatius Loyola, Saint Rita of Cascia, and Dr. Oswaldo Cruz. In his early years, Joao was often harassed by governmental and church authorities, and even jailed for practicing medicine without a license. After working as a tailor and miner through midlife, he eventually founded his spiritual hospital to dedicate himself more fully to the healing of others. Joao personally accepts no money for doing this work, although the Casa does accept charitable contributions for operating expenses and infrastructure. Joao supports himself and helps underwrite the Casa and a local food bank via proceeds from his own ranch and personal businesses.

I could not bring myself to believe the Spiritist doctrine out of hand. Why should I? I had no conscious memories or recollection of past lives, no tangible sense of being a spirit, and no contact with higher-level spirit beings, as far as I knew anyway. It's not that I'm unfamiliar with the "subtle realms." I've had myriad experiences with the unseen world and ethereal dimensions. My longtime meditation teacher and friend, Barbara, channels an entity that is an unflagging source of profound insight, wisdom, and compassion. I've had shamanic journeys in an imaginal world with animal spirits, upper world guides, deceased loved ones, and totem energies. I've used psychotropic drugs that enabled me to experience the interconnectedness of the universe, and received personal instructions in the art of living from plant medicine teachers. And I've had numerous experiences with synchronicities, premonitions, and déjà vu. But I have not adopted a particular belief system that explained such. After all, I could think of more than one possible explanation for most such phenomena. For example, what a person interprets as a past life experience could be a manifestation of *field effect*, whereby things that occur in the Universe are somehow captured in some sort of "field" that underlies all that is. Tapping into such could be misinterpreted by someone as "a past life in a stream of being." Or the person could be connecting with the transpersonal realm and collective psyche of humanity. Who knows and can say for sure? Indeed, over the last few years much of my inner work has been learning to accept that, ultimately, we live in mystery. And so I struggled with the question: "How was I going to show up in Brazil: as a believer, a skeptic, or a non-believer?"

Then, in early December, I did a breathwork session facilitated by my close friend Frank. During that session, I began thinking about the myriad explanations and interpretations people have about the nature and origin of the Universe and different belief systems. "Which belief system is correct?" I asked. And then a thought came: "They are all correct, George—*partially* correct, that is—which is why different peoples and different cultures have come to believe different things. And that partial truth is also why each system is still alive and relevant in the world today." Suddenly, I understood: I didn't need to have a belief system, an interpretation, or an opinion about any of this. Nor did I have to show up as a believer, a skeptic, or a non-believer. I could just show up "open to the experience," allowing any thoughts, feelings, sensations, and phenomena to arise. I would not try to interpret or explain them; I would simply experience them. And so I settled the issue for myself. (According to Spiritist doctrine, the Entities do not require that you believe in them. They only require that you freely ask for any healing, and that you keep an open mind about the *possibility* of their existence.)

THE CASA

On the Road (January 10 and 11)

Kris and I left Ann Arbor on Monday morning, January 10, for Detroit Metro Airport, where we joined up with Barbara. Meanwhile winter storms were pounding the southeastern United States with record snowfall and ice. Miraculously, we then flew into and out of Atlanta, even though only two of their five runways were open and over 700 flights had been cancelled there that day. Because of the storms and flight cancellations, however, we were rerouted to Sao Paulo and needed an extra flight to get to Brasilia. As a result, we didn't arrive at our hotel in Abadiania until late Tuesday evening, 35 hours after leaving Ann Arbor. It was a difficult journey.

We had an eight-hour layover in Sao Paulo. Since Barbara is a channel for an entity named Aaron, Kris and I took advantage of the time there to have Barbara ask Aaron about our karma and healings. Following are the main points that Kris (who also listened) and I remembered Aaron had to say about me:

- I often work to meet the needs of others while overlooking or ignoring my own needs.

- I get burned out because I'm not steadily connecting to the well-spring of renewal within.

- My main work is to open my heart to myself and to the divine.

- There is very little karmic material for me to work on from past lives.

I asked for Aaron's help on this because I was especially curious to know if I had any "karmic" material to work through. According to some belief systems, karmic material can result from actions in previous lifetimes. Spiritists believe that we choose to incarnate in specific circumstances for a given lifetime in order to do specific work. Even though life can unfold from there in unexpected ways (such as having a car accident or getting cancer from an environmental toxin), some of the difficulties that we experience can actually be the result of a conscious choice we made before incarnating and, therefore, is an important part of our purification work as a spirit. If that's the case, the Casa Entities may not intervene and help, as they would be interfering with a larger karmic process. As far as I could figure, my healing issues emanated from the natural tides and happenstance of circumstances occurring in this lifetime. So the mental and emotional healing I was seeking was something these healers would likely help me with.

Logistics and Accommodations

Abadiania is located on the central plain of Brazil, about 3,000 feet above sea level. A few hours drive south of the capital, Brasilia, the location was chosen by Joao's friend and mentor Francisco "Chico" Candido Xavier. He had received a channeled message directing Joao to establish a healing center in the township of Abadiania with access to a nearby waterfall. Thanks to the generosity and help of the locals, a site for the Casa was secured in a beautiful setting overlooking the surrounding expanse of hills and valleys with a nearby waterfall. It is centered over a natural energy vortex formed by quartz crystal bedrock beneath the surface. Like smaller crystals, this bedrock reputedly stores electromagnetic energy and facilitates communication. So the streams flowing out of and around these hills are believed to be a special source of healing. Because of the unusual geological nature of the area, it is considered a "portal" or place where "the veil is thin," facilitating connection to spirits for healing.

We stayed at a small hotel (called *pousada* in Portuguese) within easy walking distance of the Casa (one-half mile). I had a small, private "monastic-grade" room with a bathroom and simple furnishings, including a bed, clothing rack, a plywood shelf hinged to the wall that served as a desk, and a plastic chair. There was no television or radio. While the accommodations were spartan, the food was excellent and served buffet-style. Breakfast included coffee, tea, fruit (usually papaya and pineapple), juices, bread, butter, jam, and scrambled eggs. Lunch and dinner typically included rice, beans, chicken, a soy dish, a variety of roasted vegetables and dishes, and fresh salads. It was a very healthy and diverse array of fresh, unprocessed food.

There were 18 people in our group plus our guide, Barbara, who has been to the Casa numerous times before. She has also written and published a book about her experiences there, titled *Cosmic Healing: A Spiritual Journey with Aaron and John of God*. Barbara is a well-known and highly regarded meditation teacher. I have been her student and friend for 20 years. Her husband, Hal, is also one of my very best friends. As our guide, Barbara counseled us both individually and as a group throughout the experience. At the personal level, she tracked my journey, helped me to understand what was going on, and advised me on what to do next in this strange world of esoteric healing. As for the group, they were a wonderful mix of pilgrims and adventurers. Ranging in age from 30 years old to over 70, they were open, accepting, and caring folks, committed to healing themselves and supporting others in doing the same. As such, they naturally and spontaneously took care of one another throughout our time together.

As for Kris, she did fine, but we had a lot of problems with accessibility and her wheelchair. According to the manufacturer of her chair, the Brazilian electrical system is the worst in the world for their equipment (something we didn't learn until after we arrived in Brazil). Within the first few days, we had burned out two internal electrical converters, which are necessary for recharging the batteries. Eventually, we ended up having to manually recharge the batteries each day. This required removing them from inside the chair and using an external battery charger. Fortunately, we got by all right doing this, although Kris had no power in her chair while the batteries were being recharged. During those periods, she was totally dependent on others to push her around in the wheelchair.

Meeting the Entity (January 12)

John of God is at the Casa Wednesday through Friday. When he's not at the Casa, he spends time at his ranch or travels doing healing work. For example, he was at the Omega Institute in New York in September 2010, and was scheduled to go to Vienna in March 2011. The number of people he sees is mind-boggling. A few years ago, he saw 20,000 people over a long weekend in Peru. I read somewhere that he has personally seen and worked with over four million people. During my time at the Casa, he saw anywhere from 600 to 1,000 people a day. During the busiest times of the year there, he sees from 2,000 to 4,000 people a day. And each person comes directly before him—individually, one at a time—to request and receive healing.

And so, I ended up before the Entity on a Wednesday afternoon with about 600 other folks. I was tired from the long trip down, had slept in late, and was planning to relax the rest of the day. But Barbara insisted that I get my process underway. At the Casa, everyone stands in line to see the Entity, one at a time. There are different lines that form in the main hall, one after another, although there is no fixed order to calling them. There is the *First*

Time line, *Second Time* line, *Surgery* Line, *Revisio* line (for post-surgery), *Eight o'clock* line (morning only), and the *Two o'clock* line (afternoon only). I was in the First Time line, wearing white clothes (thereby making my auric field more visible for the Entities) and carrying a piece of paper with my written request for healing (in Portuguese).

I was asking for "complete healing of body, mind, and spirit." My deepest intention and priority, however, was for healing my heart space; that is, for "ending the war" with what is. That war is the one I continually wage by wanting things to be different from the way they are, including: people, circumstances, the weather, and my bank account. It's the war that I wage whenever I tell myself, "As soon as I change or fix this circumstance or situation, I'll be satisfied and content." It is a never-ending endeavor whereby I postpone being truly alive and open in the world, waiting for a tomorrow that never arrives. But I was advised that such a request would not translate well from English to Portuguese, linguistically or culturally. So I went with something more general that was clear and easily translatable, but still encompassed my intentions. That is, if I was truly healed in "body, mind, and spirit," I would no longer be waging my war against what is, and I would be more open to all of what Life has to offer. In any case, Barbara had pointed out beforehand that the phrasing and writing of the healing request was actually done for me, rather than for the Entity—to clarify my own intentions for healing. She claimed that the Entity would already know my request and needs from seeing and reading my heart/mind directly or firsthand.

The line filed through a doorway into the Mediums' Current room, where approximately 50 people were meditating. Sitting in several rows of pews and benches on the left, these people generate energy for the Entities to use in reading and clearing the energy bodies of the folks passing by in front of them. As I understand it, there are hundreds of unseen spirits engaged and coordinated in the work. By the time a person arrives in front of the Entity, these spirits have already determined the individual's needs and protocols for healing. People in the Current rooms are instructed to consciously offer their energy and light for healing while sitting with their eyes closed for up to four hours at a time.

The Mediums' Current room opens into a larger room that is laid out perpendicular to it, so that the two rooms together form an L-shaped space. The larger room is the Entities' Current room, which has seating for approximately 200 people. The line in that room passes up the middle of the pews, similar to the main aisle of a church. John of God is seated at the front of the room, where the line ends. Beyond that is the Surgery Room and then the exit. Shortly after I passed through the main hall doorway into the Mediums' Current room, I became very lightheaded and spacey. Then my right knee, which had been sore since the plane trip, "clicked" into place. "Wow," I thought, "They're already working on me!"

Halfway through the Mediums' Current room, my "imaginal" animal totem, Jaguar, showed up at my right side. Jaguar has appeared to me in many shamanic journeys. I remember that when I was five or six years old, I had recurring "nightmares" of a black jaguar standing near my feet on the bed. When I would cry out, my mom would invariably come into the room and assure me that the creature didn't really exist. Eventually, it disappeared from my dream world, only to reappear in my first breathwork experience 50 years later. Since then, it has shown up regularly during shamanic experiences and, occasionally, in normal waking states. In the former, it shows up whenever I call it or, sometimes, spontaneously. In the latter, it appears as a subtle presence when I'm doing something it wants to enjoy participating in. Jag asked, "Can I come to see the Entity, too?" I said, "Sure, why not." So we filed ahead together in line, side by side.

Near the front, a volunteer translator approached and reviewed my written request. Finally, we were standing before a late-middle-aged man seated in a raised chair. As the interpreter was reading my request, I felt my chest and heart explode open, thereby "presenting myself" to the Entity. It was like exposing my thoughts, intentions, personality, character, life history, and soul simultaneously—the "entire catastrophe," you might say. The Entity hardly looked at me. Instead, he rolled his eyes back and said something in Portuguese. The interpreter standing alongside me said, "Surgery tomorrow at 8 am." The entire meeting and exchange took about three seconds. I was then directed on ahead. Strangely dazed and following the person in front of me, I passed through another room where I sat to receive blessings for a few minutes, and was then ushered on outside.

With my lightheadedness and dizziness, the bright sun was overwhelming. I was directed to sit on a veranda in the shade. After a few minutes, those of us who spoke English were taken to a small room where we were counseled about the upcoming surgery. We were told to take a taxi back to the pousada after surgery, drink plenty of Casa water (which has been blessed by the Entities), and, for the next 24 hours, rest in solitude. (Contact with others after surgery is discouraged since your energy field has been opened, making you unusually vulnerable to the influence of others.)

1st Invisible Surgery (January 13)

The next day I had "surgery." That consisted of sitting in the Surgery room with about 50 other people for a short while with my eyes closed. We were each given a written prescription while being ushered into one of the pews; then we were seated and told to close our eyes and place our right hand over what we wanted healed. Or we could simply place our hand over our heart, which is what I did. As I sat there, I wondered how long we would be there as I already felt tired holding my arm and hand up. Prayers were then said aloud by the attendant, and I "zoned out." Before I knew it, we were being instructed to leave the room. I came to with my hand still resting over my heart but, surprisingly, with no sense of tiredness or discomfort. It's hard to say how long we were there, probably for no more than 15 or 20 minutes. But it is claimed that the Entities can work on a person in any dimension (physical, mental, emotional and spiritual) and at any level (including the cellular and quantum levels). And they can work on up to nine specific items or healings with a single surgery. Those of us who spoke English were again separated out for post-surgery instructions, which echoed what we were told the day before.

After that, I stopped at a kiosk to submit my personal information for having my sutures out. There, each person is requested to provide their full legal name, date of birth, and the street address at which they will be staying the 7th night after surgery (which is when the Entities supposedly return to remove the internal sutures). I then went to the pharmacy to get my prescription filled ($50 for a 70-day supply) and took a taxi back to the pousada, where I stayed in my room for the next 24 hours. Surgery restrictions included eight days with no exercise or heavy lifting, and avoiding direct sunlight. Beyond that, there are dietary and energetic restrictions when taking the prescription herbs after surgery, consisting of no hot peppers, no pork, no sex, and no alcohol or psychotropic drugs. On the 7th night after surgery, patients are supposed to wear white clothes or nothing at all, as the Entities come to remove sutures. (These "spiritual sutures" have reportedly been seen on CT scans.)

1st Post-surgery Experience (January 13 and 14)

The first 24 hours after surgery were both difficult and wonderful. I had significant lower back and kidney pain on both my flanks, and my right knee (the one that clicked) was very sore. At first I thought the back pain was due to the mattress, which was hard. But I continued to have the pain even after turning and lying on my side. Then I remembered that I have a longstanding and continuing history of kidney stones, and realized that the Entities must have worked on my kidneys. (Once you request healing from the Entities they can choose to work on any number of things, so long as it is clear to them that it would be consistent with your wishes for healing.) I also felt very tired physically, and strangely out-of-sorts mentally.

Over the next several hours I slept on and off, experiencing a sort of "slide show" that I titled, *The Worst Moments of George's Life*. These images consisted of significant moments or episodes during which I was at my worst — full of anger, mean-spiritedness, hard-heartedness, hatred, insensitivity, selfishness, cynicism, et cetera. As I lay there in bed holding a rock crystal, I witnessed these scenes unfold, feeling the ill-will or numbness of the original experience. After watching all of this for the second time, I got the message — if I wanted to heal and open my heart to the world, I had to include *all* of myself and *all* of my past, fully embracing the parts and experiences.

Alternating with the slide shows and periods of sleep, I experienced my heart space expanding far beyond the limits of my body. I had visions of a single field of love surrounding planet Earth as it sailed and spun through space. Somehow, this field of embrace seemed to originate inside of me. The sense of generating an energetic field that encompassed the entire planet was thrilling. During these periods, I would sit up in bed with a smile, radiating love, wisdom, and acceptance.

While these experiences were unfolding, I realized that my room was now teeming with animal spirits. Jaguar was lying at my feet on the bed, while other spirits milled about or rested on the floor surrounding the bed. They were all there — muskrat, bat, snake, hawk, woodpecker, squirrel, crow, hummingbird, chipmunk, raccoon, deer, turtle, mink, and others. "What are you all doing here?" I asked. "We're here to protect you," they replied. "The tree spirits would be here, too, but they can't travel like we can. Nevertheless, they appreciate your environmental work in the woodlands, and wish you well with your healing here." And so I lay there on my bed in the middle of a protective throng of animal spirits. But they were there for another reason, too; they were hoping to meet the Entities first-hand. "After all," they said, "we're from the Lower World and these healers are from the Upper World." So they hung around, partly to protect me but also to meet these other spirits.

Early on, I thought about the extraordinary range of experiences I was having—animal spirits, light-headedness, slide shows, back pains, visions, exhaustion, et cetera. And I wondered what was going on—was I imagining all of this, or was it really happening? In the end, I decided to simply allow what was occurring to unfold naturally. I would not try to stop it, control it, or interpret it. I would simply let it all happen and try to figure things out later. That would go for the post-surgery experience I was having, as well as for whatever else happened downstream. In the meantime, I decided to keep a steno book alongside the bed, making simple notations of what was occurring. Otherwise, I feared there was simply too much going on to remember. I am using those notes to write this.

Sometime before lunch, I had a strange dream. In it, I was in a large building running up several flights of stairs with a friend when I suddenly heard the Entities telling me, "No running! You have restrictions." I stopped on a landing, looking up, and said, "But this is a dream." And they replied, "It doesn't make any difference. No running." Shortly after that, soup from the Casa was delivered to my room by other members of the group, and a little while later they brought lunch. The food tasted wonderful. That afternoon, I fell asleep again and had another dream. In this one, I was in a row boat on a lake with a person very dear to me. She playfully touched me in a sexual way, and suddenly I got another message, "None of that. You're on restrictions." It was both remarkable and funny to get these lucid messages while sound asleep. In both instances, I woke up shaking my head, chuckling, and wondering how all this was going on.

Sometime during the night, I was awake in bed looking at the ceiling in the low light. We had been instructed to keep our legs and arms uncrossed. We were also advised to remain open to receive whatever healing was available, and to consciously send healing energy to others. So I was lying there doing that, holding a crystal. At some point, I blinked, and when I opened my eyes again the room was pitch dark. I blinked again, this time squeezing my eyes hard, trying to clear whatever the problem was. No luck—the room was still pitch black. Staring into the darkness, I tried to reconstruct what had been going on a few moments before. I asked myself, "Wasn't I just looking at the ceiling a few seconds ago? Why can't I see the ceiling now? Am I dreaming or awake?" I moved my body, squinted my eyes some more, and confirmed that I was definitely awake. And yes, I had just been looking at the ceiling. But no matter where I looked, there was nothing but *total* darkness. "Good grief," I thought, "These fuckers have blinded me!" But then I thought, "If I were you, George, I wouldn't be using that kind of language with these guys. And who knows, maybe this has something to do with your healing." And so I began to wonder how long the blindness would last.

Surprisingly, I was more curious than panicked. And then, as I settled into the experience, I noticed how full it was. It seemed that my other senses had suddenly become far more acute, including my sense of awareness. And I was amazed at how rich the experience was. It was entirely different than what I had imagined blindness to be like. I thought there would be a greater sense of deprivation. But that didn't seem to be the case at all; this was such a big and full experience. While my eyes had been turned "off" so to speak, it seemed that everything else had been turned "on." I wondered, again, how long this would last. Then, suddenly, I could see the ceiling again. Looking to the side, I could also see street lighting coming in through the window. Evidently, there had been an electrical power outage at the same time I blinked. Or maybe something else had happened.

People brought dinner to my room that evening and breakfast the next morning. By noon the day after surgery, I felt good enough to interface somewhat with others and take care of myself, so I ventured out to get lunch, bringing it back to my room. Nonetheless, I had a clear inner sense that I needed to take it easy, as directed. For the next several days, for example, I found the bright sun to be extraordinarily oppressive. And I had little energy for any kind of exercise or much contact with people. There was a subtle yet distinct sense of what was easy and what was difficult for me to do, and this sense was completely aligned with the restrictions people had counseled me about. It seemed remarkable that I could directly feel and sense these limits for myself, instead of having to simply accept the advice of others.

Interestingly, I discovered that I stopped biting my fingernails after surgery. While I've had the habit for as long as I can remember, I never thought to address it as part of any healing request. Still, I noticed a few days after my surgery that I had stopped doing it. (It's now several months later and I'm still not doing it.) Most important of all, I could feel that my heart space had relaxed and opened up measurably. Little did I know that this was just the beginning of the work on my heart.

The Waterfall

Over the next few days and later throughout my time there, I went to the sacred waterfall in a ravine located a half mile from the Casa. The entire area (including the waterfall, spiritual center, nearby hotels, and surroundings) is reputed to be located around a powerful energy vortex and therefore considered a portal to the spirit world. The underground crystal formations and surrounding energy field give the water a special healing charge. It is also reputed to be further energized and blessed by nature-based spirit beings there, angels drawn to the area by the Entities and their work at the Casa.

The setting is grotto-like, private, and breathtakingly beautiful—a 30-foot deep ravine, with steep walls, dense vegetation, and a 10-foot high waterfall cascading down into a small pool and stream. There are two foot bridges over the stream and rocky ledges, along with railings to hold on to for getting up to and under the falls. Over time, the water has cut its way through the rock, disappearing 50 yards or so downstream over a series of cascading granite ledges and around a bend. There are several guidelines for accessing and using the waterfall: you or the person you're with must have permission from the Entities; never go alone; males and females go separately in groups; bathing attire is required; no photographs or electronic devices; no soaps, shampoos or incense; and, no visitations from five PM to sunrise.

The water was not as cold as I thought it would be, although it was brisker on some days than on others. After periods of rain, the volume was greater and the water warmer since it was tempered by surface run-off. During periods without rain, however, the volume was lower and the temperature noticeably cooler since it was primarily sourced from underground springs. In either case, it felt exhilarating and wonderful.

Somehow, I had the good sense to consciously position myself in different ways under the waterfall. For the kidneys (which had been very sore after surgery), I sat down with my back to the waterfall and bent forward, letting the water directly hit and work my shoulders, upper back, then lower back, and flanks. For my heart space, I stood facing the waterfall and bent backward, letting the water directly hit my chest and upper torso, while visualizing that the armor there was being pulverized and broken down. Standing erect and directly underneath the waterfall, I sensed myself being thoroughly cleansed of all impurities—physical, emotional, and mental. I had visions of multidimensional detritus washing out of me and away downstream. Over time, the experience grew. On some occasions, I felt as if I were a "living tube" with experience flowing directly through me. I invariably came away from a waterfall session feeling radiant and mysteriously polished, inside and out.

Since waterfall visits were made as part of a same-gender group and only one person can use the waterfall at a time, there was time spent waiting while others were using it. After my first visit, I therefore decided to try lying in the middle of the stream bed on the rock ledges downstream of the waterfall. Not only did this also have a wonderful effect, but it enabled me to stretch the amount of time I was in the water several fold. I had powerful experiences there. Lying on my back in the rushing water, I felt as if the water was flowing both around and through me, cleansing me inside and out, physically and energetically.

Jaguar joined me on a few occasions there. First, she would walk through the stream. Then she would either climb up to lounge on a rock ledge, or clamber up a nearby tree to stretch out on a big limb in the overhanging canopy. I had never seen her experience a natural setting this way. It seemed obvious that she was quite at home there.

One time while I was lying there, a spirit-being approached me over the rocks from downstream. He came up alongside me, bent down, and offered to baptize me. After all, he pointed out, this was how people were originally baptized—in nature and totally immersed. (While *baptism* is usually associated with admission into a church, its deeper meaning and purpose is serving as an initiation and ritual for cleansing and purification.) "Sure," I said. And so I was baptized and cleansed there by a spirit-being.

On a few other occasions, late during my stay, I "saw" or sensed several faeries floating around and above me at the waterfall. They were small, hand-sized folk—like Tinkerbells—full of light and a mischievous but loving energy. I sensed them floating around and hanging along the crest of the waterfall overhead. They invariably seemed immersed in merriment. When I stepped directly under the waterfall, they would scatter a bit, floating around me giggling and laughing.

Sitting in the Current (January 19)

As described earlier, the lines to see John of God pass through the *Current Rooms*, where approximately 200 people are sitting, meditating, and praying. When sitting in Current, people are instructed to: (1) sit with hands on the legs, palms facing upwards in an open position, and with the legs uncrossed; (2) keep the eyes closed; and, (3) hold an intention of healing and love for the highest good of all. In discussions with the veterans in our group, I was also instructed to consciously generate and offer energy and light to the Entities for their healing work. By following these instructions, each person becomes a thread or link in "a chain of energy" that the Entities draw upon and use for their healing work. In this extraordinary way, everyone ends up participating in a co-creative act of healing, collaborating with the Entities to heal both themselves and others with a focus on serving the greatest good for all.

There are restrictions on coming and going to and from the Current Rooms. Basically, "traffic" is discouraged. And Current sessions can last anywhere from two to four hours. For that reason, I was quite anxious about sitting in Current. I have a weak bladder, various physical ailments (resulting from five separate knee and shoulder surgeries), and typically meditate for less than an hour at a time. Even during week-long retreats, individual meditation sittings are less than an hour and are interspersed with other activities. So I fretted about it, wondering "How on earth am I going to sit for four hours straight?" But the veterans told me not to worry. They claimed that somehow the Entities "spiritually anesthetize" people to facilitate their time in Current. Thankfully, I found this to be true.

My first time in Current, I sat through an entire morning session—almost four hours—with amazingly little discomfort. I was strategic with breakfast beforehand, minimizing liquids to avoid having to use the bathroom. I had only half a cup of coffee, no juice, and a small serving of scrambled eggs. After getting seated and settling down in the Current room, I could feel that my body was shut down in subtle ways. For example, I didn't feel or sense any movement in my digestive or urinary tracts, and the surface of my skin seemed to be less sensitive than usual. Once in while I would get stiff or achy, but a little subtle stretching easily took care of any discomfort while also giving me a surprising boost mentally. So I was able to sit relatively still and comfortably throughout the entire session, as directed; hands resting palms-up on my thighs, legs uncrossed, mentally focused on sending energy to the Entities for healing. I held a mental image of myself pouring energy out into the world. By the end of the session I felt completely empty and exhausted. Interestingly, as soon as it ended, my body came back "on line," exploding with aches, pains, and a pressing need to use the bathroom. It was like someone had flipped a switch.

During Current that morning, I received messages or thoughts that related to my own healing. I was "told" that a lot of work had been done from the *outside* to open my heart, and that I now needed to do more work from the *inside*. Evidently, my healing was to make demands not only upon the Entities but also upon myself. I also "received" a message that the earth is actually a seed of the divine. Impregnated with Life, it is a living embryo that is maturing through consciousness itself. This thought evoked a startling image for me—that of the earth spinning through space, as a distinct being and offspring of the Source.

Getting My Sutures Out (January 19/20)

I had my sutures taken out by the Entities on the 7th night after surgery. To prepare for it, I was told to do the following: (1) wear white clothing (I wore nothing at all); (2) be in bed at a reasonable hour (I was in bed at nine PM); and (3) leave a glass of Casa water out to drink in the morning. The Entities usually visit to remove the sutures sometime between one and five AM, although they can do so almost any time once you're in bed. I had no idea whether or not I had any sutures, but I did feel some very unusual tugs (for lack of a better word) inside my chest and around my heart around ten PM. I was still awake and there were just two of them, but they were distinct and unusual sensations.

Going through the Revisio Line (January 20)

The next morning, I returned to the Casa for my post-surgery follow-up. Before they formed the regular lines, however, John of God and a few staff members brought two male patients onto the podium at the front of the room to do *visible* surgeries. I happened to be with Kris that morning, near the front in the wheelchair section. So I was only 20 feet or so away from the patients, who stood facing the main hall and crowd with their backs against the wall.

Before doing the surgery, the Entity held the scalpel in his hand and slowly turned, looking around the room. Then he stopped and rested his gaze on me, as if to say, "You are one who does not believe. So watch." After fixing me with his stare, he turned back to the first patient and proceeded to cut a two-inch long incision in his chest. I could clearly see the tissue exposed below the skin. But even though it was a deep cut, the man did not appear to be experiencing any pain. He just stood there with his head tilted back and his eyes closed. Taking a hemostat, the Entity then clamped the open wound closed and turned to pick up a needle with thread that had already been affixed to another hemostat. Turning back to the man, he then proceeded to stitch the incision closed. The entire procedure took only a few minutes. There was no anesthesia or antibiotic used. (According to the literature, there has never been a case of infection resulting from physical surgery at the Casa.) Amazingly, there was only a small trickle of blood coming from the wound. The man was then lowered into a wheelchair and rolled away for recovery in the Infirmary. Then the Entity picked up another hemostat and did a nasal procedure on the second man. The hemostat was approximately six inches long, not counting the handles. The Entity inserted the entire instrument up and into the nasal cavity, twisted it around a few times and then withdrew it. Again, the person seemed to experience no pain and there was very little blood. Like the first man, he was put into a wheelchair and taken to the Infirmary. (You can see both of these procedures on the Internet at John of God's website.)

It seemed clear to me that these visible surgeries were done to convince skeptics. While the Entity saw over 550 people that morning (based on the log that the staff maintains), there were only two visible surgeries. And although people may request visible surgeries, very few do so. Some claim that the Entities work on the energetic body, at the root cause of an illness. Others claim that they work at the quantum level. In any case, my guess is that the visible surgeries help people to believe in the power of these healers. Such belief helps enhance and further the power of the healing itself. After all, the "placebo effect" is a well-known phenomenon, whereby *any* healing treatment that is believed in works approximately one-third of the time. So belief itself can be a powerful adjunct in healing.

Regardless of why these physical surgeries are done, I found the demonstration and experience to be very powerful. For me, it was a tangible and extraordinarily convincing demonstration that *spirit* does exist—a mystery that lies beyond the physical world that we can see and measure. And there was a sense that more about this mystery will be revealed after death. That possibility gave me a new outlook on *death*. While I previously viewed death primarily as an *ending*—losing that which I cherish and merging back into the Cosmic flow—now I saw it more as a *doorway* into the mystery itself. So a new part of me came to life around death, a part that is both curious and anticipatory about what's in store for me beyond the threshold. This felt remarkably healing, leaving me with a deeper sense of peace about my life and situation.

Later that morning, I joined the Revisio line for my post-surgery check-up. When I arrived in front of the Entity, he said "Come back at two this afternoon." After lunch, I returned to the Casa and joined the 2 o'clock line. I was then told, "Surgery tomorrow." So I returned to the pousada, looking forward to having surgery again the following day. As Barbara noted over dinner that evening, this is probably the only place in the world where everyone says, "Great!" when you tell them that you're having surgery.

2nd Invisible Surgery (January 21)

I returned to the Casa in the morning for my second surgery. After a few opening prayers and invocations, the Surgery line was called. About 50 of us filed into the Surgery room, where we were each given a written prescription and ushered into our seats. I placed my hand over my heart and began to hold intentions for my healing.

After a few minutes, I "heard" my deceased mentor Bill Bottum, "George, where have you been? I've been trying to contact you. Remember when I said that we needed to figure out a way for us to communicate when I'm dead? And I gave you the book on *kything* to read?" Of course, I remembered. The conversation had been extraordinary. He was the only person in my life who wanted to strategize about post-mortem communication; that is, how we were going to communicate with each other after he died. I realized that my loss of connection with him in the spirit realm was another symptom of how my heart had closed. After that, I noticed that the animal spirits had re-joined the party, milling around me and occupying the open floor of the Surgery room. They seemed amazed and in awe of whatever they could see and sense. Later on, they relaxed and seemed unconcerned about any need to protect me.

After surgery, I got my new prescription filled and then took a taxi back to the pousada. I was back in my room around nine AM.

2nd Post-surgery Experience (January 21 and 22)

Like the first surgery, I was exhausted afterward. For the next 24 hours, I alternated between periods of sleep and wakefulness, while experiencing unusual physical sensations, insights, and visions. I noticed this time, however, that only Jaguar was in the room, lying on the bed at my feet. Evidently, the other animal spirits were satisfied with their early-morning encounters in Surgery and no longer thought I needed any protection.

When I was awake, I felt light-headed and spacey but mentally alert. Nevertheless, I was too tired and out-of-sorts to sit up in bed. So I lay there, with my arms and legs uncrossed and my feet hanging over the end of the bed. For a while I placed a crystal over each of my chakras while meditating, opening to receive while sending healing to others.

Early on, I went through an experience and laundry list of "Things I Need to Forgive Myself For." It covered a wide range of heartbreaking phenomena, along with their gut-wrenching consequences, including broken relationships, objectification of women, not wanting to have children, judging others, substance abuse, killing animals, et cetera. It included the missing story lines and text for the slide shows I watched after my first surgery. And it was *generic*; that is, I sensed the underlying pattern of each incident, rather than just noting the particulars of the incident itself. As a result, I understood that each one actually represented a *class* of others, encompassing a pattern and body of experience that closed the heart and created its own particular form of darkness. Once again, the message seemed to be for me to open my heart to myself. "The war that you've waged hasn't just been against what's *out there*, George, but also against what's *in here*." The message was, "Love it *all*. Heal yourself, and then heal the world." I didn't realize it at the time, but this last admonition represented a subtle but important shift in the work.

Besides the mental and emotional work on my heart, I also experienced some strange physical sensations. First, I again had severe pains in my kidneys along both flanks. By now I knew that this had nothing to do with the bed mattress. So I figured that the Entities were working on my kidneys. Second and even more unusual, I felt strong pulses of energy going through my body. These entered through the crown of the head, flowed down through the torso, and exited straight out the soles of my feet. I experienced several of these pulses over a period of five or ten minutes. After that, I sensed that some sort of "knot" had released over my heart, as if a big fist that had been clenched there was suddenly relaxed. It was a subtle but pleasant sensation, filling me with a sense of grace and ease. I was very grateful for it, and gently excited that the heart work was continuing.

Lastly, I had thoughts about the physical surgeries I had seen the day before. For me they were evidence that spirit *does* exist, that there is much more going on than meets the eye. Most importantly, there is "something" that lies beyond death. And even though this something remains a mystery, it is enough. "Great!" I thought.

By now, I had learned to give myself over to the exhaustion that seemed endemic there. There were odd times of the day when all I wanted to do was sleep. Since I had experienced and seen enough to trust the process, I surrendered to the tiredness and took frequent naps. This dynamic continued for almost two months after I returned home.

Sitting in the Current (January 26 and 27)

I sat in the Current again for a four-hour session on Wednesday and a three-hour session on Thursday. Lengths of the sessions vary, depending on how many people need to be seen, how much energy is being generated in the Current and is available for healing, the particular Entity that has incorporated that session in Joao, and who knows what else.

As before, I had no problem with having to urinate or use the bathroom. Somehow these normal functions were shut down or suspended for the duration of the sessions. However, I did have a lot of difficulty with my "sit bones" on Wednesday. They became sore and achy, and moving or shifting around a bit gave me only a moment or so of relief. I thought I might have to excuse myself from the session early. After experiencing the discomfort and fidgeting for a while, I asked the Entities, "Help me out here. If I don't get some relief I'll have to leave." A few minutes later, I somehow got the idea of contracting my buttock muscles. This required using only the upper part of my lungs to breathe, since my diaphragm was engaged with holding the buttock muscles. After doing this for five minutes or so, I released the contraction and literally "sailed" into an easy, open meditative space of comfort and expansion. From then on, and during future Current sittings, I used this method whenever my buttock muscles felt achy. It worked remarkably well, freeing me up from discomfort for half an hour or so at a time. There were other occasions when the Entities seemed to help, too. A couple of times, I fell asleep for just a few minutes. When I awoke, I had the thought, "That was a rest for you, George. Now re-focus. Offer your energy for the healing of others."

Going through the Revisio Line (January 28)

I returned to the Casa and went through the morning Revisio Line for my post-surgery check-up. The Entity told me to take two crystal baths and told Kris to take one, too. Because of concerns with wheelchair access for Kris, we checked out the facilities together, and then scheduled appointments for early afternoon. I scheduled my baths after hers, so that I could be available to help her with transfers.

At this point, I couldn't help but notice that the Entities were prescribing Kris and me the same treatments. She had surgeries on the same days that I did, and now we were both having crystal baths on the same day. I wondered if they were keeping us together so that I would be available to help her if needed. Of course, I had no way of knowing whether or not this was true. But every other person in Barbara's group at the pousada had a unique route of treatment, except for Kris and me. Ours had been the same. This actually worked out really well since we had to manually recharge the batteries in her wheelchair, which required a fair bit of synchronization with our schedules.

The Crystal Baths (January 28)

Crystal baths are prescribed by the Entities for energetic alignment, rejuvenation, and/or preparation for more healing work. The person receiving the "bath" lies face up on a bed with eyes closed, under an array of seven quartz crystals. The position of the crystals is adjusted so that there is a specific crystal suspended over each of the body's energetic centers. These centers, called *chakras* from the Sanskrit word for "wheel," reputedly spin the body's energy through the nervous system. They are located and aligned along the spinal column, from the base of the spine to the top of the head. Each crystal has been cut to emit a specific frequency for a particular chakra, and has a colored pulsing light behind it that also corresponds to that particular chakra. The pulsing array creates an alternating energetic pattern that clears, balances, and amplifies the person's vital energies. In addition, the Casa spirits are also reputedly engaged with the process. Once you are on the bed, the attendants turn off the light and leave the room. Sessions are regularly scheduled for 20 minutes each in private rooms.

Because of transfer issues with Kris, we had scheduled her session first, followed by mine. That way I could be available for getting her onto and off the crystal bed. My two sessions were scheduled after hers, back-to-back. By so doing, I had hoped to deepen the experience. After getting Kris settled on the crystal bed, I took a seat on the veranda outside her room overlooking the surrounding grounds. People were sitting on benches or strolling the walkways. I settled into a relaxed, easy state watching the park-like setting in front me.

Then I began to have a vision, or hallucination, with my eyes open. A horse and rider came into view floating across the grounds and approached me. As they got close, the rider pulled the horse to a stop, dismounted, and squarely faced me. He wasn't wearing a helmet, but he did have some sort of chain mail on with the hood pulled down and draped across the back of his shoulders. Somehow I recognized him as King Arthur of the Round Table. He turned back to the horse, drew a long sword from a scabbard on the saddle, and then turned to face me again. Stepping nearer and standing over me, he raised and lowered the sword twice, touching each of my shoulders in turn. Then he declared, "You are hereby a Knight of the Round Table."

Behind and to the right of Arthur was a large, round table, sitting in the middle of the grounds—obviously, *the* Round Table—with several knights and nobles around it. They were at various angles of repose, sitting or standing, some with their backs to me. One of them sitting on the near right side had his chair half-turned my way and I recognized him immediately: my friend and mentor Bill Bottum. He was looking straight at me with a slight smile and gleam in his eye, as if to say, "Well, didn't I tell you?" (While visiting London on business once, Bill took a side trip searching southwestern England for the Round Table of King Arthur.) Alongside Bill were two empty chairs, which I somehow knew belonged to King Arthur and me. Then Arthur said, "You incarnated to carry on the work of the Round Table, and to bring the Council of Equals into the world. It is work that we share. You now need to write your book about it. I will help you." (Note: During my career, I helped design and implement a participatory governance system—called the *Council of Equals*—that was nationally recognized for its innovation and effectiveness.) With that he turned away, slipped the sword back into its scabbard, and mounted the horse. Pulling the reins, he turned and rode slowly away across the Casa grounds, the Round Table fading away behind him.

I sat there wondering what had just happened, asking myself if the experience was real. I tried to recall "how" I was able to see it, with my eyes open no less. The whole scene and experience was like watching a projection on a piece of glass between me and consensual reality. The images seemed phantom-like. But I was not just *watching* the experience, I was actually *living* it. As I sat there bewildered, the attendant returned to open Kris's door and I got up from my chair to help.

After getting Kris back into her wheelchair, I entered the room next door for my own crystal bath sessions and got myself situated. There is a roll of sanitary paper at the head of the bed, so that users can have something clean to lie on. I pulled fresh paper down over the bed and lay down face up with the crystal apparatus suspended above me. Then the attendant stopped by to make sure everything was OK, turned a fan on in the room for me, and closed the door behind her as she left. I covered my eyes with a towel that was available and wondered what was going to happen next. Since I had scheduled myself for back-to-back sessions, I knew that I would be there for about 45 minutes.

I lay there following the usual instructions; arms and legs uncrossed, opening to receive healing, and sending energy out to the world for others. After a while, I began to sense a weight or heaviness on my chest, directly over my heart. At first, I assumed it was just another phenomenon related to the healing work. So I returned to my meditation on opening and sending. But the sense of weight on my chest grew stronger. While I knew that I was alone in the room, there was a palpable sense that someone or something was physically weighing down on my chest. I raised the towel from my eyes and lifted my head to see what was going on. What I "saw" were several faeries sitting on my chest, casually hanging out, apparently oblivious to the deeper work that was supposedly going on. I thought, "Hey, give me a break here. I'm trying to open my heart space. And you're sitting on it!" They turned and looked at me. Then one of them said, "Silly boy, the heart opens from the *inside* not the *outside*." With that, my chest exploded open, sending the little people tumbling and somersaulting through the air and around the room. It was as if a heavy stone slab had been blown away from the top of a vault, leaving a gaping hole into the chamber below. The faeries seemed to think that all of this was great fun—they floated and circled around the room, giggling and laughing. Then they re-convened around the hole, sitting along the edge with their feet dangling over it.

After that, things calmed down and not much happened. Time began to stretch, so much so that I began to think the allotted time had elapsed and the staff had forgotten about me. Not so. After a bit, the door opened and the attendant entered to help me get up and exit the room.

Distant Healing

As noted earlier, I took healing requests for 30 people with me to the Casa and the Entities. This required submitting an individual photo of each person (ideally, dressed in white) with their personal data written on the back (full legal name, nickname, date of birth, address, and requested healings). There are two options that people have for doing distant healing work with the Entities, which I will refer to the *Blessing Mode* and the *Herbal Mode*. Of the requests that I was carrying, 16 were for Blessing Mode and 14 were for Herbal Mode.

Blessing Mode

The Blessing Mode entails submitting a request for blessing and healing. This requires providing a photo of the person (dressed in white) along with some personal information on the back (full legal name, nickname, date of birth, address, and healing requests). These requests are then placed in the bottom of a large wooden triangle located on the front wall in the Main Hall over the platform or stage. When that is full, a medium removes them and takes them to the Entities. During my visit to the Casa, I submitted the 16 requests for Blessing Mode a few at a time. For each one, I would: (1) think about the individual, (2) put their photo and request into the triangle, and (3) say a short blessing or benediction from a *Lovingkindness Meditation* taught by Barbara and Aaron. This invariably brought tears to my eyes. The blessing goes:

> ~~May you be free from suffering.
> ~~May you be happy.
> ~~May you love and be loved.
> ~~May you find the healing that you seek.
> ~~May you find peace.

Herbal Mode

The Herbal Mode entails a bigger commitment and more involved process; requiring more participation on the part of the person requesting the healing, and giving the Entities greater access to the mind and body for doing their work. In this mode, the person's photo and personal information are submitted directly to the Entities. After reviewing those, they write an herbal prescription for the individual which is filled at the Casa pharmacy. While taking the herbs, the person is requested to abide by the following restrictions: (1) no hot peppers for food intake, (2) no pork, and (3) no alcohol. These restrictions apply throughout the time taking the herbs, which is a minimum 40 days. In rare cases, the Entities do not prescribe herbs for a person. Occasionally, in very serious cases, they recommend that the person come to Brazil where there are greater resources available for the work. They indicate the latter by drawing an "X" over the photo.

I took all 14 of the healing requests for Herbal Mode together with me into the Second Time line on Friday, January 28, after doing my crystal baths. I had "stewed" about these requests for several days, wondering if I should take them all at once or in smaller batches of a few at a time. I was concerned about holding up the line with so many requests, as well as getting the prescriptions mixed up. But due to my own healing process (which included two surgeries and related restrictions), I didn't have many opportunities to get these requests processed. In any case, I ended up taking and submitting all of them at the same time. Because I was concerned about holding up others behind me in line, I waited to step in at the tail end of the Second

Time line in the afternoon. Then I realized that the 2 o'clock line would be called and formed behind me, so I would be holding other folks up regardless. After stepping into line, however, my thinking and outlook changed dramatically. Somehow, I got the sense that the Entities were appreciative and delighted that I carried so many requests with me. I began "hearing" thoughts like: "Thank you, George, for bringing these healing requests to us on behalf of so many. That is why we are here. We are grateful to help." With thoughts like these, I suddenly felt wonderful as the line moved ahead, and I became quite excited about helping so many family members and friends.

Arriving at the front of the line, I immediately felt disoriented and spacey. As he slouched in his chair, the Entity's eyes and demeanor radiated a powerful sense of connection and unconditional love. I felt an immediate sense of recognition, like I was greeting an old friend. And even though he had already seen almost 1,000 people before me that day, he was entirely fresh and present. Feeling such unconditional love and presence, I spontaneously fell to one knee at his feet and started weeping. The Entity took the photos from the interpreter. Looking at each one in turn, he wrote a script and then went on to the next one, carefully keeping the photos and scripts together in order.

While the Entity was doing that, he began talking to me. First he said, "Male and female crystals would be helpful for you." Then he asked, "How long will you be at the Casa?" I told him two more weeks. "I will help you," he replied. (This inferred that he had not been helping me previously, a clue that I was meeting a different spirit than before.) Then he said, "And you will be coming back here. Now sit in my Current." With that, he finished the photos and scripts and handed them back to the interpreter, who then handed them to me. I carefully put the pile of documents into my backpack, and then seated myself in the Entities' Current room for the reminder of the afternoon session. I was thrilled. I had the prescriptions. The Entity had made a tangible, specific commitment to help with my healing. And he had invited me to sit in his Current. (Afterward, based on descriptions of the numerous Entities that incarnate through Joao, I surmised that this was the spirit or energy of Oswaldo Cruz, a German doctor and famous healer. He and his colleagues developed the vaccine for Yellow Fever.)

The following Wednesday (February 2) Kris got all the prescriptions filled for me at the Casa pharmacy. Each script was bagged separately, and included six containers of herbs (having 35 capsules each) along with the individual's photo and healing request. I then labeled each container with the person's initials to avoid any possible mix-ups in U. S. Customs when we re-entered the country.

More about the Restrictions

There are reasons for the restrictions. Related to pork, pigs do not have a lymphatic system, which functions to remove cellular debris and toxins from the body's circulatory system. Pork, therefore, is more likely to be contaminated with toxins and chemicals that undermine the healing process. And, of course, alcohol is a toxin. Lastly, by making such temporary adjustments in our personal lives, we become active partners in the healing process itself. People can choose to start the restrictions immediately after committing to making their request, or they can begin when starting the herbs. The earlier a person starts the better, but individuals need to be on the restrictions throughout the time they are taking the herbs which is a minimum of 40 days.

More about the Herbs

The herbs consist of passion flower (*Passiflora*), as commonly used in herbal teas. It is completely safe, has no known side effects, and no contraindications when used with other medications. The Entities give a unique blessing to each prescription, thereby tailoring it to needs of the individual. So while each prescription is made from the same herb in the same dosage (210 mg), it is *energetically* different. A 60 to 70 day supply of prescription herbs costs approximately $50. Barbara told me that the herbs enable the Entities to gain greater access into the mind and body. So there is supposedly much to gain by taking the herbs and doing the restrictions. Curious, I asked Barbara what the relative strengths of the different healing modalities are. As a rough estimate, she rated them as follows on a scale from 1 to 100: (1) the Blessing Mode would be a 40, (2) Herbal Mode a 70, and (3) personally coming to the Casa 100+. So while there are definite advantages for doing the herbs and/or going to the Casa, each of the healing modes is quite powerful.

Whether individuals chose the Blessing Mode or the Herbal Mode, I encouraged them to participate in their healing experience by incorporating intention and ritual. Specifically, I suggested that they do the following two or three times daily:

Step 1. Sit or lie down quietly. Consciously decide to dedicate the next few minutes to your own healing. Then take three slow, deep breaths.

Step 2. Feel or imagine yourself opening to receive whatever healing the universe has to offer you.

Step 3. Visualize yourself sending healing energy to the myriad others in the world who are also in pain.

Two of the best times to do this are before getting out of bed in the morning and after getting into bed at night. Lastly, I recommended that people continue with the protocol for several months. I have followed these guidelines myself beginning two months before I left for Brazil.

Sitting in the Current (January 28)

It had already been a "big day" for me. I had been visited by King Arthur, taken back-to-back crystal baths, had a stone slab that covered my heart chamber removed with the help of faeries, obtained herbal prescriptions from the Entities for my friends and family, and been invited to sit in the Entities current. Not bad. And so I seated myself mid-afternoon in the Entities Current room, feeling excited and somewhat bewildered with everything that had happened.

But the show wasn't over. While I sat there, Arthur slowly rode up the aisle from behind me. Pulling his massive mount up alongside the pew, he stopped, leaned over, and looked at me. Then, confirming and reinforcing our earlier encounter, he slowly said, "The Council of Equals is a spiritual archetype. Remember the work you incarnated to do." With that, he straightened back up, reined his horse forward and rode on up the aisle, fading away in front of me. Later on during the session, I "received" the following message: "Make your inner work and journey the highest priority in your life. Never compromise it."

Sitting in the Current (February 2)

I sat in the Current again for, thankfully, a relatively short session, less than three hours. Most importantly, Arthur showed up again to continue his work with me. He and another spirit-being—Dr. Oswaldo Cruz, I believe—removed a massive door from an interior wall surrounding my heart. With the door on the ground, they turned to me and said, "Remember, nothing—absolutely nothing—is worth covering or shielding the heart. Not even to protect yourself from pain or loss." Then they dragged the door through the opening to inside the wall, and on across an open landscape to a large hole at the center of my being. This pit, or crater, was filled with a strange white fire burning with a singularly large flame. Somehow, I knew the flame had no temperature but would consume whatever it touched. Standing alongside the crater, Arthur and Dr. Cruz lifted and pushed the door over the edge. It did a slow-motion somersault into the flame below and disappeared without a trace.

Dismantling the Wall (February 3 and 4)

The next day, I woke up with a sense that the spirits had been working on me while I slept. Closing my eyes and "looking" inside, I saw that they were now dismantling the interior wall that surrounded and somehow enclosed my heart. There was a large, jagged opening with felled stones and blocks lying about, encompassing and stretching well beyond the old door opening. And there were various beings engaged in the work—including Arthur, Dr. Cruz, a host of faeries, and animal spirits—all taking down the wall around my heart. The faeries were removing stones and blocks one at a time, knocking and pushing them out of the cracking mortar until they tumbled to the ground below. Interestingly, the size of a piece was proportional to the loss I had experienced. There were small, common bricks for minor losses, and large stones of granite for major losses. The largest stones bore names of loved ones who have passed—Virginia (my mom), Carl (my best friend), and Bill (my mentor). The faeries were blessing and de-energizing each brick and stone, thereby releasing the embodied pain and completing the experience that had been arrested. After that, the animal spirits would push the brick or block along the ground and into the open pit at my center. The largest ones were being moved by Arthur, Dr. Cruz, and—believe it or not—some elephants. The steady white flame vaporized anything and everything that fell into it.

For the next 24 hours, work continued on dismantling the wall. When I awoke on Friday morning, it was completely gone. The spirit beings who worked on it were also gone. Lying there in bed before breakfast, I surveyed the inner landscape and open crater with its white flame. Suddenly the landscape itself began to slowly shift and dissolve, collapsing around the crater's edge and crumbling into the flame. As that happened, the flame grew to fill the vacuum left behind, thereby occupying more and more of the inner space of my body. Soon, everything was gone but the flame. When I looked inside, there was neither landscape, nor wall, nor door, only a bright white light that started just on the other side of my skin and went deep within. I sensed that this light went on forever, possibly, all the way to the Source.

Trajectory of the Healing Adventure

With these latest phenomena, I began to see more clearly the evolution of my healing adventure with John of God and the Entities. While each pilgrim undoubtedly has his or her own unique journey, I found that there were three distinct phases to mine.

> *Phase* I. At the beginning I was concerned with curing physical ailments and emotional disorders, thereby ending my pain and suffering. I thought I knew what I needed and asked for it, more or less self-managing my own process. The emphasis was on the remission of specific symptoms. At this stage I asked the Entities for "total and complete healing."

> *Phase II.* After encountering the Entities and personally experiencing their work, I started to question how much I really knew about healing. Then my focus shifted—from being concerned with specific symptoms to being at peace with myself and my life. I began to suspect that my original healing request was symptomatic of a deeper unseen "dis-ease," and that I might not know what I truly needed to be healed. I eventually came to believe that I could trust the Entities—or whatever was going on—to manage my healing process on behalf of both myself and the greater good. So at this stage I asked the Entities, "You know my needs. Where do you want me to go?"

> *Phase III.* By now, my focus and outlook had changed dramatically. Even though I was still "symptomatic" in many ways at one level (the mundane), I felt whole and complete at another level (the spiritual). Here, I discovered—or rediscovered—

my calling and vocation. I was no longer so much concerned about fixing and healing myself, but about pouring and emptying myself into the world on behalf of others. In this stage, I acknowledged and embraced the gifts I was carrying to further the greatest good for all, thereby becoming a healer myself.

And so, I was not being *cured* so much as being *healed*. And not just for myself, but for the greater good of all.

As we neared the end of our month-long trip, Kris and I began wondering how we could "stretch" or continue our healing journey after getting back home, which many folks claimed is possible to do. So during our last week in Brazil, we dialogued about how to do that. Through those discussions and some personal reflection, I developed an initial outline for what I came to call "The Work."

1. Make *The Work* life priority #1.

2. Abide in "the Center," as witness.

3. Keep the heart space open and clear.

4. Engage on what has meaning and purpose.

5. Sustain and nourish myself.

As best as I could figure, these tenets encompassed the major experiences, stages, and principles that had played out during the journey. And to sustain that journey, I set a strong intention to compass my life around them. But I still needed to clarify things. Specifically, I needed to understand what a daily practice would look like. Although I didn't know it at the time, I would have to live into that understanding rather than figure it out. And that would take me several months to do.

Returning Home (February 7)

A week before we were scheduled to return home, Kris asked me if it would be all right to return earlier than planned. She had had enough—physically, mentally, and emotionally. The ongoing complications with her wheelchair, coupled with the intensity of her healing experience, had worn her out. So we made plans to return a few days early, leaving on Monday instead of Friday.

We had a fitful start to our trip home, with our taxi for the airport arriving three hours late. But we still managed to catch our scheduled fight out of Brasilia, and had an uneventful trip the rest of the way. For two weeks afterward, however, I was plagued with extremely low energy. I worked only a few hours each day, typing up notes from the trip. The rest of the time I spent napping and reflecting on the experience. After a few weeks, I was able to slowly begin re-engaging with my life as normal.

While I had a new sense of life purpose and direction, there were outstanding commitments I had made before the trip. Primarily, we had already scheduled a busy retreat and workshop season at Sunnyside [the retreat center and homestead where I live and work as a part-time caretaker and host] for spring 2011. The busy schedule and some major repairs required my working almost full-time from mid-February through mid-June. Nevertheless, I remained committed to continue with *The Work* with whatever time was available.

Beyond that, I had no interest in most anything else. That included things such as politics, hobbies and diversions, television, vacation cruises, home improvements, the stock market, great deals, new stuff, professional sports, and gossip. On the one hand, this enabled me to stay focused and get traction on *The Work*. On the other hand, it meant that I had little or no interest in what occupies most people.

At this point, I assumed that the "fireworks" were over, at least in terms of my extraordinary encounters with these healers or energies. But I could not have been more mistaken!

LIVING DOWNSTREAM

Sharing the Notes

By late February, I had typed up the first round of my notes from the trip and begun sharing them with a few friends and others who expressed interest. While I initially wrote them to help me understand and integrate my experience, they turned out to be an easy way to respond to folks who wanted to know about the trip. So when people asked me about it, I typically declined to discuss it much and emailed them the notes instead. This saved a lot of time, and everybody got the same information and story.

People generally reacted to the notes in one of two ways. In the "first camp" were people deeply moved and affected by the material, and there was a surprising number of them. These folks typically shared that the notes somehow resonated with them. And they often remarked that they intended to read them again. Some asked for permission to share the material with others, which I freely gave. A few wanted to meet and discuss the adventure further with me, which I declined to do. It seemed that my calling wasn't to delve further with others into the experience, but to continue on with the experience itself; simply doing *The Work*. Also, I thought that I could best help others not by further exploring and fixating on *my* journey, but by role modeling and encouraging them to undertake *their own* journey — the one that only they could do — which would understandably be different from mine.

In the "second camp" were folks that I never heard from again. No kidding. And who could blame them? Much of the claimed and shared experience falls far outside the acceptable limits and boundaries of conventional mores and consensual reality. These folks neither confirmed receiving the material nor commented on it. Through third parties, I learned that a few of them were genuinely concerned about my mental health and well-being. But so was I. After all, my journey has been away from mainstream society and conventional programming. I walked away from a secure job and career without adequate financial resources for retirement, abandoned a loving relationship with a wonderful partner, now work at a small retreat center as a host for little or no wages, eschew conventional social contact, and sleep outdoors in a tent most of the year. With all of that as context, my latest foray could easily be viewed as (choose one): going over the edge, falling off the deep end, flipping out, or having a total meltdown. So to be honest, even I am concerned about the trajectory of my life. In fact, I often wonder, "What the hell am I doing? Where is all this going to end up?" And of course, the old cliché, "I sure hope that I don't become a burden to my children."

Council of Equals Presentation (March 4)

The first week of March, a month after returning from Brazil, I presented a workshop on the Council of Equals at a conference for college and university executive officers and educators in Indianapolis. I originally planned on dedicating the session to Bill and Arthur. But the night before the presentation, I awoke at three am with the thought, "Instead of dedicating the session to us, why not list us as co-presenters? After all, we'll be there helping you." That made perfect sense. So I got up from bed, changed my Power-Point presentation to show and credit Bill and Arthur as "co-presenters," and then went back to sleep.

With my session scheduled for mid-morning and the room available beforehand, I had plenty of time to test drive the audio/visual equipment (the Achilles Heel for presentations) and then settle into a state of acute-but-not-paralyzing anxiety. This nervousness has invariably been the case for me before presentations and workshops.

Using the bathroom to take a whiz just before the session, I suddenly sensed Bill on my left and Arthur on my right, alongside me. As a thought in my mind, I then "heard" Arthur say, "Hey, George, don't worry. We're here … Didn't I tell you I would help?" I stood at the urinal, facing the tiled wall, and zipped up my pants. Then I shook my head, trying to clear it. I took a mental step back—out of the experience, so to speak—trying to check whether or not this was really happening. Was it was real or imagined? I couldn't tell! At one level, I could not visibly see or physically touch either Bill or Arthur. But at another level, I had a distinct sense that they were there with me. Similar to seeing Arthur on the grounds at the Casa, it was like watching a projection on a piece of glass between me and consensual reality. I could "see" gossamer-type images of Bill and Arthur alongside me even though I knew they weren't visibly there.

I washed up and left the bathroom, continuing to feel their energies. As I walked down the hallway, images flashed through my mind—first *The Three Musketeers*, then *The Blues Brothers*, and then *The Matrix*. With that, I envisioned the three of us striding together down the corridor, shoulder to shoulder, arms and feet in lockstep, wearing black dusters and dark sunglasses. "Cool!" I thought. Amazingly, my nervousness had vanished. Instead, there was a sense of exhilaration and love. In four decades of public speaking experience, I had never felt so relaxed and at ease before a speaking engagement. So I thought, "Wow … This must really be happening, at some level anyway. Otherwise I wouldn't feel like this." Then I thought, "Terrific … Let's go with it."

I entered the room feeling ebullient; playful rather than nervous. Walking to the front, I shook hands with the fellow who was there to introduce me to the audience. He welcomed folks to the session and went through the perfunctory "blah-blah" and accolades about my work, even though it was obvious—at least to me—that he was completely unfamiliar with any of it. After he finished, I thanked him and everyone for being there, told them what a gift it was for me to be able to share about the Council of Equals, and proceeded to introduce my two co-facilitators—Bill Bottum and Arthur Pendragon. At that point, some of the folks began to turn and look around the room for these guys, as they obviously weren't standing with me at the front. I said, "You probably can't see them right now, but I can assure you that they are here—not physically, but *other-dimensionally.*"

After introducing Bill, I began introducing Arthur. "Most of you are already familiar with Arthur Pendragon, not under his common name but under his historical moniker—King Arthur … of the Round Table." I stopped momentarily for folks to take this all in. A few of them fidgeted a bit. After all, there had already been a strange beginning to the session and now it was getting even stranger. I continued, "Historians generally agree that King Arthur was not a single individual. Rather, they claim that he was a *mythic composite* of several individuals who led the Brits against foreign invaders during the 5th and 6th centuries. Interestingly, that is consistent with what the legends claim. That is, Arthur was not a single *person*, he was a single *spirit*. And that spirit has incarnated—or embodied—in different lives at different times. According to these same legends, he and his band of Superheroes sleep in caverns deep in the hinterlands between incarnations, waiting for their next call … And so I am now calling upon Arthur to be with us here today." It's stupefying for me to realize that I said this outrageous stuff to a group of executive officers and educators from colleges and universities. But I did.

Notwithstanding my craziness, the session was well-received. With only one exception, the evaluations had the highest possible scores for presentation style and session content. The single exception rated my style as "low" or "poor," most likely reflecting the fact that I was operating outside the conventional bandwidth of acceptability. Afterward, the Executive Director of the organization that sponsored and organized the conference contacted me. He had attended the session and was very interested in further supporting the Council of Equals work, including finding other presentation venues for me and publishing a related essay if I was willing to write one.

More Instructions

Shortly after the conference, I was treated rather inconsiderately (or so I thought) by someone whom I had supported over the years with both my time and energy. While sitting in meditation the next morning, the incident came to mind and I thought, "Fucking bullshit!" And off I went, distractedly replaying the incident in my mind while anger and resentment grew inside me. Suddenly, the following thoughts came: "George … Use the white light … In the words of your world, it is like a *nuclear furnace*. It can vaporize whatever you release into it … Send this negative thought into the light, along with any resentment and ill-will."

I sat frozen still, mesmerized. Then more thoughts came: "Do this with *any* negativity that arises within you … This light was our gift to you. Not just for healing your past, but also for managing your present and creating your future … Stay vigilant … Use the light." And so I turned inward with my mind's eye—toward the light—sending the dark thought and ill-will into it. Sure enough, they disappeared and my mind went blank. I felt an immediate sense of release and ease.

Sitting there, I realized what should have been obvious before. While I can empty and cleanse my heart space of negativity and contractedness about the past, I remain vulnerable to accumulating more such negativity through experiencing and processing the present. So I need to be ever-vigilant; watching the mind and consciously responding to whatever negativity and ill-will arise.

Next, I began wondering what had happened, asking myself, "Did the Entities just pay me a visit? Was that some sort of *transmission* from them? …

Or did I access an archetypal pattern within the psyche? ... Or, maybe, I somehow connected to a repository field of energetic wisdom?" And lastly, "This is nuts! I probably just dozed off while meditating and dreamt it." But I didn't have *any* sense of dozing off. And regardless of the explanation for what had just occurred, I knew that I had just received—or happened upon—a wise and powerful instruction. While I didn't know *what* was going on, I knew that *something* was going on. And whatever it was, it resonated as an authentic part of the journey I was on.

As I closed the session, I refocused on the theme and content of the message itself—releasing and letting go of ill-will and negativity. Then I wondered, "Could it really be possible for me to end the tyranny of contraction around my heart? Could I simply let go and love everyone and everything?" I thought, "Maybe." And then I thought," Freedom!"

So I began using this technique for negative thoughts and feelings that arose, especially ill-will and resentment. As soon as I was aware of them, I stopped and consciously released the negativity into the light. It invariably vanished and my mind would go blank. But it wasn't always a permanent fix. With more significant experiences, the same thought or feeling would usually reappear, perhaps later that day or the following week. In those cases, I would simply release it again ... and again ... and again, until it finally lost its "charge" or no longer showed up. Like repeatedly pulling a weed without getting to the root, the shoots became smaller and smaller until they no longer appeared.

The Brothers and Sisters of Light (March 16)

The following week, Barbara brought a group to Sunnyside for *personal retreat*. In this kind of format or venue, people spend their day in solitude— meditating and doing inner work. They meet with the teacher for only a short time each day (15 to 30 minutes) to check in and get further instructions. Beyond that, they are on their own. As host and caretaker at Sunnyside, my job is preparing the meals and addressing any housekeeping and maintenance items.

Midway through the week-long retreat, Barbara told me that they were going to do a group meditation in the boathouse after lunch, and that there was a good possibility that "The Brothers and Sisters of Light" would show

up. According to her, these spirits are different from the Casa Entities channeled by John of God, since they come through a different medium. These
other spirits or energies visit her often and have asked to be called *The Brothers and Sisters of Light*. But the essence of one's experience with them is similar—having direct contact with a *source* or *beingness* that encompasses time-
less wisdom, universal love, and potential healing. Since I had journeyed to
Brazil with her, Barbara invited me to join the group for the session. But I
was already scheduled to work in the kitchen with a neighbor, Sylvia, whom
I had asked over that day for help. Not wanting to leave Sylvia alone with
lunch clean-up after asking for the help, I told Barbara that I would pass.
But to tell the whole truth, there was another reason. Besides the consid-
eration for my generous neighbor, I was embarrassed about drinking beer
since returning home. Even though I had reduced my more-than-adequate
intake of the brew since returning from Brazil, I knew that it was still too
much and was therefore hesitant to present myself. So this was also at work
in my declining the invitation.

After lunch, the group retired to the boathouse as planned for their session,
while Sylvia and I cleaned up the kitchen from lunch and started preparations for dinner. A short while later, one of the guests returned to the kitchen
and said, "George, the spirits are asking for you. They want to check how
your surgery is doing." My heart stopped. "Well," I thought, "I guess there's
no getting around it." I put down my dish towel, asked Sylvia to excuse me
for a bit, and left the kitchen. Descending the outside steps toward the boathouse, I felt lightheaded and wondered, "Is this really happening?"

I crossed the boathouse deck and pushed the door partially open. Lean-
ing my head through the doorway, I peered into the space. The day-lit
room was quiet. Barbara—or Barbara's body—or the entity—or whatever—
was seated in a chair opposite the door, looking straight at me. The others
were scattered about the room on pillows and furniture, with their heads
turned and facing the door expectantly. It was clear that I was the next item
on the agenda.

The look on Barbara's face was different from usual—with squinting eyes
and a furrowed brow. She was obviously "incorporated," her ego and per-
sona withdrawn from the body and replaced by some sort of entity or other
energy. In a deeper-than-normal voice for Barbara, this other said, "Please

come in, George. I see that you are *hiding* from me." I thought, "Shit, these guys can see everything!"

I entered the room feeling anxious, not knowing what was going to happen. Then I closed the door, walked across the room, and sat on the floor directly in front of the entity, looking up into its eyes. As I held the gaze, my mind raced along frantically, wondering how to react to the situation. The options seemed simple enough. I could either: (1) try to fake my way through this, or (2) open to the experience and "this other." Somehow I decided on the latter. And so, nervous and embarrassed, I gradually "lowered the shields" and opened into transparency, letting my *entire personal catastrophe* (what I call, "the George Project") be scrutinized—thoughts, feelings, memories, fears, fantasies, regrets, hopes, and history—beer drinking and all. As I did so, I felt a wonderful, non-physical warmth flowing into me.

The face and eyes of this other—or entity—softened. The head tilted and a gentle smile slowly appeared. Holding my gaze, it nodded knowingly, as if to say, "Yes, I can see you now." Then, surprisingly, the entity chuckled softly, apparently bemused by seeing what I had been embarrassed about. After that, the entity said, "Please stand up. I want to check how your surgery has gone." So I stood up. The entity stood, too. Then this other placed its left hand on my chest over the heart. Next, it reached around behind me and placed its right hand on my lower back over the spine. After a bit, the entity said, "Good ... Very good ... It is going well." Then the hands dropped.

And there we were, silently facing each other—in a fishbowl, so to speak—with everyone else around us looking on. I was transfixed, fascinated by what was happening. Time stood still. Even though a boiling sea of thoughts, feelings, and emotions churned up inside of me, I somehow felt suspended there, watching it all. After what seemed like a long time but was probably no longer than two or three minutes, I blurted out, "Who are you?" The entity's gaze intensified. And the eyes narrowed, as if trying to penetrate and reach a deeper part of me. Then it said, "The name is not important ... but I am a *spirit-brother* of yours ... and you know me." Somehow, at some level, I sensed this was true. I *did* know this one. And I knew that he—or she—or it—or whatever it was—was truly there to help me. I bowed my head and said, "Thank you."

Next, a remarkable thing happened. The entity replied, "You are welcome … Thank you for coming to see me … I *deeply* appreciate it." With that, I felt an incredible wave—or pulse—of love and gratitude flow through me, emanating from this other. So powerful that it actually felt physical. After that, it settled and stabilized into some sort of energetic field that filled both myself and the space around me. In that moment, I think I glimpsed what it feels like to live in the open heart. And with that glimpse, I realized how far away from there I live in my contractedness.

Then, suddenly, it was over. A palpable sense of absence—or emptiness— fell upon the room, like someone had thrown a blanket over it. There was nothing there, neither spirit nor energy. I turned and walked out of the boat-house, my mind swimming with questions. "*What* is 'going well'?" And, "What did these guys learn by putting Barbara's hands on me that way? What did they see?" Then it hit me—I had not even thought to ask such questions. "Too bad," I thought, "because they probably would have been answered." Ultimately, I found some solace in having enough sense to ask at least one good question. And the answer was intriguing, to say the least.

Using the Longbow (April 5)

In early April I did another breathing session with Frank. It was a walk-in format that he conducts in a group setting on Tuesday mornings. During the session I found myself in another dimension or realm, one that I've often vis-ited during breathwork and shamanic journeys. I was originally introduced to this realm by Jaguar almost a decade ago. It is a phantasmagorical place inhabited by animal totems and spirit energies. The landscape is varied and rich. There is dense jungle pierced by a river that has waterfalls, sections of whitewater, and still pools. There are caverns and caves in the surrounding craggy hills, one of which I use for shelter and ceremony with the animal spirits. And there is a higher-level valley of lush grass surrounded by distant mountains. While journeying in this realm, I am free to travel throughout the terrain, usually accompanied by Jaguar and other totem energies. And I am lucid during these journeys; I can write notes, use the bathroom, or even stop the journey if I choose.

After getting activated with the breathing, I found myself and Jaguar in the upper valley. We were walking through knee-high grass toward a small hill. Suspended high above us was a *cosmic sun*—a rotating, pulsing vortex of golden light. Along its perimeter, glowing streams of energy were spin-ning off and raining slowly downward to the horizon below. These rivu-lets flowed through the mountains and on into the surrounding landscape, eventually giving rise to and animating the myriad forms we call Life. With the decline and passing of these same forms, the shimmering energy reap-peared, condensing out of matter and streaming its way back upward into the center of the pulsing orb. The overall effect was a stunning and vibrant tapestry of dynamic interconnection and wholeness.

Walking along there with Jag, I impulsively wanted to introduce and share this extraordinary place with Bill and Arthur. They immediately appeared alongside me, Bill on my left and Arthur on my right. I said (or thought), "Greetings guys. I wanted you to see this place." After that I was quiet, as this realm could speak for itself. And so we walked on together in silence, swishing our way through the long grass.

After a bit, Arthur spoke up. "George, have you ever shot an English long-bow?" Turning toward him, I noticed a strikingly large bow on his back, the end of which was a couple of feet above his head. We all stopped. Arthur pulled off the bow and stood it upright, planting one end in the ground at his feet. Even so, the upper end of the stave was still more than a foot above his head. Reaching across the front of himself with his free hand, he pulled a long arrow from a quiver at his side. Then he notched it, drew the bow back while turning and sweeping upward toward the sky, and let fly the shaft. With a quick shudder and strange hum, the arrow rocketed away from us. Shielding our eyes to look up, Bill and I followed the arrow's long, arching flight across the sky until it eventually—and astonishingly—disappeared into the center of the pulsing sun.

We stood there awestruck. Arthur turned slowly back toward us, grinning. After waiting a moment for us to fully take in what we had just seen, he began telling us about the legendary power of the longbow. "This is an amazing instrument," he said. "The larger ones have a range of 300 yards." "But," I exclaimed, "that arrow went all the way into the sun!" "Well, yes," he replied, "in *this* realm its range is probably unlimited."

Then, with increasing excitement, he said, "Now look, George. Look at what you can do." He put down the bow, took another arrow from the quiver, and reached around behind me to pull a marker from my backpack. Squatting down, he laid the arrow across the front of his thighs and wrote something along the shaft. Then he lifted and held it in front of me, so that I could read what he had written. It was the name of someone who had recently "pissed me off." The memory flashed up, along with a twinge of anger and contractedness. Bending down and picking up the bow, he notched the inscribed shaft into the bowstring. With a twinkle in his eyes he looked back and forth, from me to Bill and to me again. Then he turned, drew and raised the massive bow in an upward sweeping motion, and loosed it again. Like the first, the arrow broke the air with a shudder and rocketed away, streaking along a great arching path toward the golden bulls-eye above. As it disappeared there, I felt an immediate sense of relief and ease.

Turning back to us, Arthur continued. "So George, you can use this longbow for letting go of *any* negativity. All you have to do is visualize being here, inscribe the shaft, then shoot it into the sun. And you can write most anything. Works great!" He went on further, "Why, you could even do a *life review* and shoot a quiver-full if you want." Thinking about how many arrows that might take, I asked, "Well, how many arrows does the quiver hold?" Getting my drift, he replied, "Don't worry, George. In this realm, the quiver will never run out of arrows. Indeed, it will probably always seem full." Still not satisfied, I asked, "What about wrist snap? I hate that." Arthur raised his eyebrows and silently held my gaze for a moment, implying that the answer should have been obvious by now. Then he slowly replied, "That won't happen in this realm."

The Meditations (April and May)

Around this time, I began working with two guided meditations—*Pointing Out Instructions* and a *Lovingkindness Meditation*:

> *Pointing Out Instructions.* These kinds of meditations facilitate experiencing the part of ourselves that is aware. They are antidotes to getting caught up in the mundane, thereby facilitating a sense of connection to our deeper nature and "the wellspring within." The meditation I cobbled together was based on the work of some terrific teachers, primarily Connierae Andreas, Catherine Ingram, Gangaji, and Ken Wilber.

Lovingkindness Meditations. These kinds of meditations facilitate opening the heart. They are antidotes to contracting around pain and suffering, thereby enabling us to stay open to whatever Life has to offer. For the most part, the one I crafted was based upon different versions done by my teachers, Barbara and Aaron.

I had previously worked with each of these meditations on and off over the years, adapting them to fit my current needs and predicament. But after resurrecting and working with them again for a few weeks, I had an "Aha!" moment and realized they were integral to *The Work.* In hindsight, it is obvious; *Pointing Out Instructions* to abide as witness, *Lovingkindness* to open the heart. (Both of these meditations are included in their entirety in the next section.)

Throughout April and May, I did the *Lovingkindness Meditation* at least once or twice a day. Some days, I did it more often. Early on I just read it slowly, which takes about 45 minutes. I also frequently made notes and revised it several times to smooth out the "road bumps." After a while, I pretty much had it committed to memory. Then I could—and would—recite it almost anytime and anywhere, even while driving the car. All of this made a noticeable, positive difference in the quality of my life. With my mind and heart so occupied (sending loving intentions and blessings into the world), there was significantly less mind chatter. This naturally resulted in less judgment and ill-will, which settled me into a more loving and peaceful state of being. And the more time that I spent in this uplifting space, the less prone I was to abandoning it.

After I had been doing this practice for a month, something surprising happened. I began to spontaneously recite a shorthand version of the meditation whenever ill-will arose. For example, if someone did something that made me angry, the following thoughts would automatically come to mind:

Look more deeply at this one … See that he (or she) has suffered, too. Known pain of the body, mind, and heart. Experienced illness, loneliness, and despair. Felt confused, alone, and afraid … Now offer this one blessings: May you be free from suffering. May you be happy. May you be at ease.

This *tape* would start playing in my head as soon as I began to feel ill-will toward another. Simultaneously, mental images would arise depicting the transience of Life, reminding me that each of us—including this difficult one—is destined to die and leave everything cherished behind. The effect was powerful. Even though there was usually plenty of reason to be angry or upset with this other person, I was invariably brought back to a place of ease and openheartedness. Not in a way that left me vulnerable to any abuse or such, but in a way that simply recognized the reality of the other without harboring any ill-will or resentment.

Rolling It Up

We finished our busy spring retreat season at Sunnyside in mid-June. After that, I began working steadily on the second round of these notes, incorporating what had happened since I returned from Brazil and explaining how I had come to do *The Work*.

Sitting here now and sifting through it all, I am struck by: (1) the extraordinary and unfathomable nature of the experiences; (2) how the healings and outcomes aligned with my intentions and goals for the trip; and, (3) how the stages and sequence of the journey itself turned out to be a road map and prescription for daily living.

Making Healing a Priority

The first step of the journey was setting an intention and making a commitment to my own healing. This entailed bringing healing to the foreground and consigning everything else—*everything*—to the background.

Abiding in "the Center" as Witness

Next and early on at the Casa, I was somehow "enabled" with an elevated capacity to see—or *witness*—a wide range of personal issues, attributes, and ego-based patterns. This capacity included a remarkable sense of ease and equanimity with whatever came up. So even though the things coming up were about "me," they didn't feel personal; they seemed more like manifestations of basic humanity, rather than defining characteristics of mine. So I was remarkably free of related contractions, what psychologists call "secondary afflictive states" (such as, feeling bad about being a *jerk*). Instead of stewing about what came up, I simply noted it and placed it on an imaginary table set out buffet-style with other dishes of my mental and emotional stuff. After a few weeks, the table was full with most everything problematic in my life. But somehow, I was able to gracefully bear and accept it all. And while I realized that I could keep anything that I wanted to defend, the will to do so often fell away under the gaze and equanimity of the *witness*. This capacity and process was curative for a lot of what I saw there.

Eventually, I came to understand that this *witness*—or awareness—is part of my most essential nature and lies deep inside of me. And it has been watching my entire life; silently witnessing the "in here" (my thoughts and feelings) and the "out there" (the external world). Yet, this awareness remains mysteriously unaffected by the passing parade. Even more mysterious, its gaze somehow undermines and heals a lot of the problematic stuff that it witnesses.

As near as I can figure, this *witness* or "Center" of awareness is what the sages and mystics have been pointing at throughout the ages and around the world. While they have had different names for it (including the *Seer*, the *Kingdom of Heaven*, the *soul*, and the *Beloved*), the basic nature of the experience they describe is similar: a silent witnessing—or atmosphere—or beingness—characterized by a profound sense of equanimity, peace, acceptance, oneness, wisdom, and love. Interestingly, this very experience was the ultimate goal of the negative aspects that I was witnessing. In other words, my compulsive tendencies, bad habits, neurotic fears, generalized anxiety, self-defeating behaviors, negative self-talk, and various forms of addiction, are all strategies that my mind/body system uses and employs to get to the same place—a sense of OKness, peace, and love. And yet there it was, already shining in the very core of my own being, just as the sages claim, "closer than my own breath."

Under the gaze and knowingness of the witness, my negative behaviors and tendencies were seen for what they are: well-intentioned but misguided attempts to realize inner peace and freedom. Not only that, they are conditioned phenomena; arising and passing, based upon circumstances and conditions. But the witness itself is not conditioned; it is changelessly present. More to the point, "cooked" in the sanctuary of the witness, negative symptoms can melt or fall away; like icicles dripping in the warm sun, or leaves dropping from a tree after a full summer.

Opening the Heart

After I gained access to the *witness*, the ego-based infrastructure I had erected over the years around my heart was steadily—and fantastically—dismantled. That involved opening up to the darker parts of myself and personal history; releasing some sort of energetic knot or fist clenched around my heart space; removing a heavy stone slab covering the chamber; and, taking down a massive door and stone wall surrounding the core. After that, the interior of my body was dissolved and then filled by a white light and flame, emanating from my innermost being.

These and other astounding experiences comprised a multidimensional extravaganza of energetic, psychological, emotional, physical, imaginal, and metaphorical healings. But it didn't stop there. After getting back home, I continued to have extraordinary experiences for healing into openheartedness. These included receiving specific instructions for releasing negativity and ill-will into the core light within. With that, I came to realize that this inner light not only served to heal the past, but was also available to manage the present and shape my future. I also received instructions for releasing ill-will and negativity in non-ordinary reality; using a longbow, no less, to shoot an inscribed arrow into a cosmic sun. But regardless of the reality—ordinary or non-ordinary—the message was clear: sustaining the open heart requires constant vigilance and steady practice. It's a full-time job, "24/7" as they say.

Finding Meaning and Purpose

After getting grounded in the *witness* and opening my heart space, the journey moved on to life meaning and purpose. That's when Arthur showed up. His appearance and call for me to promote the Council of Equals and participatory governance were life-giving to me. Even if the visionary experiences I had of him were illusions or hallucinations, they made life worth living. After all, the meaning of something is derived from its relationship to a greater whole. And I wanted something greater to live for than just myself, something beyond self-interest and mundane needs. So I am called to work on the Council of Equals and dedicate myself to furthering its cause. I am also called to do more writing about the inner journey, Servant-Leadership (a philosophy and movement based upon creating a more just and loving society), and other subjects that further a greater good for all. These endeavors will be the bigger projects of my life in mainstream society.

Being Sustained and Nourished

Throughout the experience, I was sustained and nourished in myriad ways—physically, emotionally, mentally, and spiritually. First and foremost, there was a palpable atmosphere of love and support for me throughout the trip, with especially heartfelt connections to Barbara, Aaron, and Kris. The general atmosphere at the pousada, the Casa, and its surrounding environs was also extraordinary; saturated with love and populated with caring people, spirit-beings, and/or healing energies. Even the food was nourishing. Along with all of that, I was cleansed, purified, and polished by immersions in a sacred waterfall and crystal baths.

My original goals for the journey were threefold. First, I wanted to help make it feasible for Kris to travel and see John of God at his Brazilian sanctuary. Second, I wanted to serve as a courier for family and friends by carrying and submitting long-distance healing requests on their behalf. And third, I wanted to "end the war" against what is, open my heart, and renew myself to better serve my family and others in the years ahead. Amazingly enough, each of these goals was for the most part fulfilled. I was able to help Kris get there and back. I carried and delivered healing requests on behalf of others. And I made significant inroads on my own healing—coming to more fully accept what is, open my heart, and find a renewed sense of life meaning and purpose.

It's been almost a year since the journey began with my decision to go, and over half a year since I returned home. Oftentimes now, I have an invigorating sense that this is, as they say, the first day of the rest of my life. And I am grateful for that. But every once in a while, I get an even stronger sense—that I'm an arrow loosed from Arthur's longbow, rocketing across the sky high above, traveling a long and graceful arc back toward Source. May it be so.

THE WORK

The Work

After returning home, I spent several months trying to better understand and integrate what I had learned. I was particularly interested in stabilizing and, if possible, expanding my sense of: (1) the *witness*, (2) openheartedness, and (3) life purpose. So I put together a practice regimen for *The Work*. The related principles and tenets are consistent with the major spiritual and wisdom traditions. They can be applied by most anyone—regardless of belief—and you don't have to go to Brazil to do it. After spending the last several months establishing a daily practice for such, I share the framework on the following page for those who may be so interested.

Of course, the principles therein are nothing new. As already noted, they have each been a thread in the fabric of various spiritual traditions over the millennia and around the world. But my Brazilian adventure brought them together in a new way for me, where they were woven into a unique tapestry and guide for daily living and healing.

I find it fascinating that the experience contained the blueprint—or DNA—for sustaining itself, and that the stages and sequence of the experience can be used as a prescription for daily living and healing. As that slowly dawned on me, I began asking myself, "Is there more going on here than meets the eye?" After all, one of my intentions and goals for making this journey was to serve as a courier in service to the healing of others. That is why I carried healing requests to Brazil on behalf of others and brought back herbs for them. And so I wonder: "Did the Entities—or energies—or whatever—also have me bring back something for everyone else; namely, this manuscript and *The Work*? ... Is that what's going on here? ... Is that possible?" And the thought comes, "Of course it's possible, George."

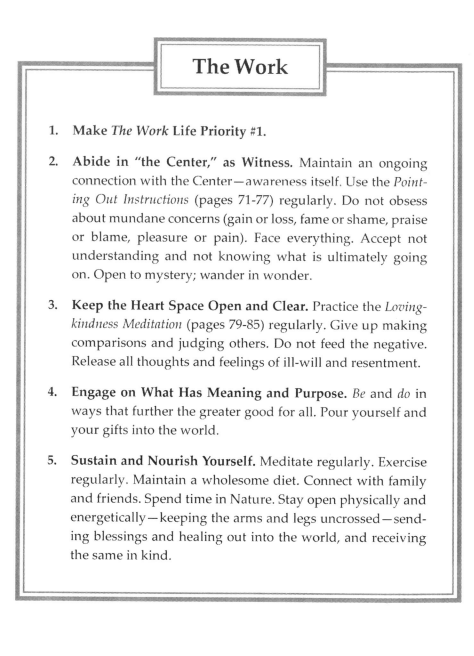

The Work

1. **Make *The Work* Life Priority #1.**

2. **Abide in "the Center," as Witness.** Maintain an ongoing connection with the Center—awareness itself. Use the *Pointing Out Instructions* (pages 71-77) regularly. Do not obsess about mundane concerns (gain or loss, fame or shame, praise or blame, pleasure or pain). Face everything. Accept not understanding and not knowing what is ultimately going on. Open to mystery; wander in wonder.

3. **Keep the Heart Space Open and Clear.** Practice the *Lovingkindness Meditation* (pages 79-85) regularly. Give up making comparisons and judging others. Do not feed the negative. Release all thoughts and feelings of ill-will and resentment.

4. **Engage on What Has Meaning and Purpose.** *Be* and *do* in ways that further the greater good for all. Pour yourself and your gifts into the world.

5. **Sustain and Nourish Yourself.** Meditate regularly. Exercise regularly. Maintain a wholesome diet. Connect with family and friends. Spend time in Nature. Stay open physically and energetically—keeping the arms and legs uncrossed—sending blessings and healing out into the world, and receiving the same in kind.

Pointing Out Instructions

This guided meditation is about experiencing the part of you that is ***aware***. *It is an antidote to getting caught up in the mundane (including your thoughts, feelings, habits, ego, and personality). And it can reconnect you to an unchanging and ever-present source—or atmosphere—of peace, wisdom, and love. It is based upon and adapted from the work of Connierae Andreas, Catherine Ingram, Gangaji, and Ken Wilber.*

The meditation can be read aloud or silently. Most importantly, it needs to be done ***slowly***. *So be sure to pause in the spaces indicated by … (for a short pause) and by … … (for a longer pause). Beyond that, there is no right way or wrong way to do the practice.*

As you work with this meditation and practice, feel free to modify it and make it your own.

Find a comfortable, sitting position; body relaxed, back erect, eyes closed softly. After settling in for a moment, proceed as follows.

- Become aware of your breathing …

- Take three complete breaths—breathing in and breathing out …

- Next, make time in your life to do this meditation … Set aside your concerns. Tell yourself that when the meditation is over you will take care of whatever needs to be addressed. But for the next while—beginning right now—you are going to focus exclusively on the meditation.

- Now, return to your breath … Watch and feel it moving in and out of your body. Notice your stomach rising and falling …

- Relax … …

Now, think back to a specific time or circumstance when you were a child or adolescent …
Perhaps you were playing outside.

Maybe you were doing something special.
Or, maybe it was a special occasion.
In your mind's eye, visualize yourself then ...

What was your body like?

... ...

What were your life circumstances?

... ...

What did you think about the world?

... ...

OK, now think about yourself today ...
What is your body like?

... ...

What are your life circumstances?

... ...

What do you think about the world?

... ...

Now, compare these responses with your previous ones ...

Aren't they different? ...

Isn't your body different? ...
Aren't your life circumstances different? ...
And what about your thoughts about the world? ...
Aren't they different, too? ...

Isn't it true

that throughout your life
most *everything* has changed? ...
your body ...
your life circumstances ...
your thoughts about the world ...
Haven't they all been in a state of flux?

... ...

Is there *anything* about you that has remained the same?

... ...

What about the part of you that is *aware*? ...

The part of you that has been "watching" all these years ...
just watching ...
without commentary or judgment ...

The part of you that watched when you were a child ...
and is watching right now ...

Isn't that the same? ...
this awareness ...
this *seer* ...
this *witness* ...

Hasn't it been the *only* constant in your life,
besides *change* itself? ...

always watching ...

silently witnessing ...

And *notice* ...
this awareness is unblemished and unmarked ...
completely clear ...

All of the millions of thoughts and feelings

that have passed through this awareness
over the course of your life
are now gone ...
totally gone ...

Of course, there may be more thoughts and feelings arising as you read
or hear this,
but they'll be gone, too ...

So this awareness is completely free ...

You can see the truth of this for yourself ...
nothing is sticking ...

Thoughts go by ...
Feelings go by ...
The natural world goes by ...

Yet, this awareness ...
this deeply inward part of you ...
remains free and clear ...
just watching

... ...

This core of being—or atmosphere—is changelessly present ...
always there ...
always available ...

... ...

The dictionary defines the word *essential* as,
"the unchanging and most important characteristic of something" ...
Isn't this awareness—this witness—the most *essential* part of you? ...
Unchanging? ...
Your most important characteristic? ...

... ...

Now, if you can, **NOTICE** ...
This *place*—or *atmosphere*—or *beingness*—is filled with some extraordinary qualities.

- There is a sense of **WAKEFUL STILLNESS** ... being at rest and completely aware in the moment ... Like a deep lake, still and clear ...

- a sense of **PEACE** ... free of worry and anxiety ...

- a sense **OKness** ... and **CONTENTMENT** ... with no need to have or do anything ...

- a sense of **EASE** ... free from mind chatter and the tyranny of the psyche ...

- a sense of **EQUANIMITY** ... an even-minded witnessing to everything that arises ...

- a sense of **SPACE** ... big enough to hold the entire parade of Life arising and passing by ...

- a sense of **ONENESS** ... where boundaries tend to dissolve ... and you see how apparently separate things connect and flow into one another ...

- a sense of **WISDOM** ... and **CLARITY** ... that sees through the clutter of daily thoughts and stories ...

and ...

- a sense of **LOVE**, without an object ... what is called "**UNCON-DITIONAL LOVE**"

... ...

This is what the sages have been pointing at,
throughout the ages and across the traditions ...
that which is always present ...

Not surprisingly, they have different names for it:

- The Chinese Zen patriarchs called it "the face you had before you were born" ... and "your Original Face" ...

- Hindus call it "the Seer" ...

- Sufis refer to it as "the Beloved" ...

- Jesus called it "the Kingdom of Heaven" ...

- Buddhists refer to it as "Original Mind" ... and "Buddha Nature" ...

- Some call it "the I-am" ...

Other names for it include:

- presence ...

- radiant, free consciousness ...

- soul ...

and

- the witness ...

Whatever the name, the sages say that
it is *closer to you than your own breath* ...

And they *universally* claim
that it is nothing less
than the *manifest essence* of who—or what—you really are ...

So the sages have been calling you ...
to see *what is shining in the core of your being* ...
right here, right now.

... ...

Allow yourself to spend a few more moments here ...
abiding in *what is always present* ...
resting in the *deepest water* of who—or what—you really are ...

... ...

As you open your eyes now,
the room or space you're in
will flood back into your vision ...
But this *awareness*—or *Kingdom*—or *witness*—or *atmosphere* ...
will still be present ...
and closer to you than your own breath ...

Lovingkindness Meditation

This guided meditation is about opening your heart to all beings—including yourself—and wishing them well. It is an antidote to contracting around the pain and suffering of Life, which separates us from others. It is based upon and adapted from the work of Barbara Brodsky and Aaron.

*The meditation can be read aloud or silently. Most importantly, it needs to be done **slowly**. So be sure to pause in the spaces indicated by ... (for a short pause) and by ... ... (for a longer pause). Beyond that, there is no right way or wrong way to do the practice.*

This is an exercise meant to be grounded in peace, acceptance, and non-violence. You are therefore requested to enter it only as deeply as is comfortable for you. If resistance arises, simply note it and continue the meditation in whatever way you are able.

As you work with this meditation and practice, feel free to modify it and make it your own.

Find a comfortable, sitting position; body relaxed, back erect, eyes closed softly. After settling in for moment, bring your attention to your breath and proceed as follows.

- Become aware of your breathing ...

- Take three complete breaths—breathing in and breathing out ...

- Next, make time in your life to do this meditation ... Set aside your concerns. Tell yourself that when the meditation is over you will take care of whatever needs to be addressed. But for the next while—beginning right now—you are going to focus exclusively on the meditation ...

- Now return to your breath ... Feel it moving in and out of your body. Notice your stomach rising and falling ...

- Relax ... ...

Now, bring to your mind and heart the image of someone that you love, someone who is precious to you. This may be a family member, a friend, a mentor, anyone that you love and hold dearly. Imagine that individual standing in front of you ...

Looking deeply at the person, see that he or she has suffered ... Felt pain of the body, mind, and heart. Known illness, loss, and fear. Felt confused, lonely, and afraid ... See some of the many ways this dear one has known pain and suffered.

... ...

Speaking silently from the heart, acknowledge this one's pain. Addressing them first by name, tell them:

> I know you have suffered ... You have not been able to protect yourself from what has harmed you. Nor have you been able to hold on to what you have lost ... You have known illness, loneliness, and fear. You have felt your heart contracted and closed ... Life has not always given you what you would have wished for, and so you have suffered ...

Now send this dear one your loving thoughts and intentions. Speaking again, silently from the heart, offer them the following blessings:

- May you be free from suffering ...
- May you be happy ...
- May you love and be loved ...
- May you find peace ...
- May you be at ease ...

Repeat these blessings again, slowly. There is no hurry ... Allow your heart to connect with this dear one in lovingkindness. Synchronize your breathing, using one in-and-out breath for each blessing.

- May you be free from suffering ...
- May you be happy ...
- May you love and be loved ...
- May you find peace ...

- May you be at ease ...

Continue silently in this way for a while.

... ...

Now invite your own self into this heart space, entering and coming to stand alongside the one you love.

Because it is sometimes hard to open our hearts to ourselves, it may help to see yourself as a young child or adolescent ...

Bring your mind's eye to rest softly upon yourself ... Observe that, just like the loved one, *you* have suffered too ... Felt pain of the body, mind, and heart. Known illness, loss, and fear. Felt confused, lonely, and afraid ... See some of the many ways you have known pain and suffered ...

Speaking silently from the heart, acknowledge this pain. Addressing yourself by name first, tell yourself:

> I know you have suffered ... You have not been able to protect
> yourself from what has harmed you. Nor have you been able to
> hold on to what you have lost ... You have known illness, loneliness, and fear. You have felt your heart contracted and closed ...
> Life has not always given you what you would have wished for,
> and so you have suffered ...

Now send yourself loving thoughts and intentions. Speaking silently from the heart, offer yourself the following blessings:

- May you be free from suffering ...
- May you be happy ...
- May you love and be loved ...
- May you find peace ...
- May you be at ease ...

Repeat these blessings again, slowly. There is no hurry ... Allow your heart to connect with yourself in lovingkindness. Synchronize your breathing, using one in-and-out breath for each blessing.

- May you be free from suffering ...
- May you be happy ...
- May you love and be loved ...
- May you find peace ...
- May you be at ease ...

Continue silently in this way for a while.

... ...

Now bring to mind someone who has been difficult ... Someone with whom you do not feel connected. Rather, you feel distant, hurt, or angry. Perhaps you feel ill-will toward this one. Nevertheless, invite him or her into this space ... In your mind's eye, see this one joining and standing alongside yourself and your loved one.

Looking deeply, deeper than you have before, see that this one has suffered too ... Felt pain of the body, mind and heart. Known illness, loss, and fear. Felt confused, lonely, and afraid ... See some of the many ways this one has known pain and suffered ...

Speaking silently from the heart, acknowledge this one's pain. Addressing them first by name, tell them:

> I know you have suffered ... You have not been able to protect yourself from what has harmed you. Nor have you been able to hold on to what you have lost ... You have known illness, loneliness, and fear. You have felt your heart contracted and closed ... Life has not always given you what you would have wished, and so you have suffered ...

Now send this difficult one your loving thoughts and intentions. Speaking silently from the heart, offer him or her the following blessings:

- May you be free from suffering ...
- May you be happy ...
- May you love and be loved ...
- May you find peace ...

- May you be at ease ...

Repeat these blessings again, slowly. There is no hurry ... Allow your heart to connect with this one in lovingkindness. Synchronize your breathing with the blessings, using one in-and-out breath for each.

- May you be free from suffering ...
- May you be happy ...
- May you love and be loved ...
- May you find peace ...
- May you be at ease ...

Continue silently in this way for a while.

... ...

Now bring to mind the many people that you have known in this lifetime. Invite them all into the space in front of you. In your mind's eye, see them streaming in from all sides to join and stand around yourself, your loved one, and the difficult one ... Take a moment to scan the gathering and to recognize some of the many faces that have inhabited your life—family members—playmates—neighbors—classmates—friends—co-workers—and others.

Looking upon this *Gathering of Familiars*, see that each of them has suffered too ... They have felt pain of the body, mind, and heart. They have known illness, loss, and fear. Felt confused, lonely, and afraid ... See some of the many ways they have known pain and suffered ...

Speaking silently from the heart, acknowledge this pain. Tell them:

> I know you have suffered ... You have not been able to protect yourself from what has harmed you. Nor have you have been able to hold on to what you have lost ... You have known illness, loneliness, and fear. You have felt your heart contracted and closed ... Life has not always given you what you would have wished for, and so you have suffered ...

Now send these people your loving thoughts and intentions. Speaking silently from the heart, offer them the following blessings:

- May you be free from suffering ...
- May you be happy ...
- May you love and be loved ...
- May you find peace ...
- May you be at ease ...

Repeat these blessings again, slowly. There is no hurry ... Allow your heart to connect with this *Gathering of Familiars* in lovingkindness. Synchronize your breathing with the blessings, using one in-and-out breath for each.

- May you be free from suffering ...
- May you be happy ...
- May you love and be loved ...
- May you find peace ...
- May you be at ease ...

Continue silently in this way for a while.

... ...

Now bring to mind the rest of humanity, as well as *The Others*—the plants and animals that make up the rest of Life on earth. Picture these beings coming and joining the gathering from all sides, surrounding yourself and the others already there ... See them streaming into the space in front of you—people from Africa, Asia, Europe and the Americas ... two-legged and four-legged animals ... the winged ones ... aquatic beings from the oceans ... creatures from the insect and reptile realms ... trees from the Plant Kingdom. Picture them all coming in to surround and join those already there, including the dear one, yourself, the difficult one, and the many people that you have known ...

Bring your mind's eye to gaze and rest softly upon this *Gathering of All Beings* ... See that pain is part of life, and realize that each being standing before you has felt pain and suffered ...

Speaking silently from the heart, acknowledge that pain. Tell them:

I know you have suffered ... You have not been able to protect yourself from what has harmed you. Nor have you been able to hold on to what you have lost ... Life has not always given you what you would have wished for, and so you have suffered ...

Now send this *Gathering of All Beings* your loving thoughts and intentions. Speaking silently from the heart, offer the following blessings:

- May you be free from suffering ...
- May you be at ease ...

Repeat this several times. Allow your heart to connect with this multitude in lovingkindness ... Synchronize your breathing with the blessing, using one in-and-out breath each time you recite them.

- May you be free from suffering ...
- May you be at ease ...

Continue silently in this way for a while.

Now close the meditation with three complete breaths—breathing in and breathing out ...

Acknowledgements

Thanks to …

Frank Levey, for the breathwork sessions. Sandy Wiener, for encouraging and supporting the writing. Anna Marie Henrich and Jack Koepfgen for the crystal baths.

Kris Kurnit, who got me to go on an adventure I would never have done otherwise. Barbara Brodsky and Aaron, for serving as trail guides. Bill, Arthur, John of God, and the Entities—or energies—or whatever—without whom there would not have been much of an adventure at all.

Dorothy Lenz, for doing the lion's share of the editing. Roann Altman, for final corrections and polishing. Alex SanFacon, for book layout and cover design. Hal Rothbart, for publishing expertise and support.

With love and gratitude,

George

About the Author

George SanFacon has worked as a grocery clerk, painter, maintenance mechanic, custodian, security guard, high school teacher, short-order cook, facilities engineer, energy conservation consultant, trainer, facilitator, operations director, management consultant, and executive coach. While an administrator at the University of Michigan, he pioneered and implemented a participatory approach to management and governance—the Council of Equals—that was nationally recognized for its innovation and effectiveness.

George is the author of *A Conscious Person's Guide to the Workplace* (available through Amazon.com), and co-author of the essay, *Holistic Servant-Leadership* (available free online at www.spearscenter.org).

George lives and works as a part-time caretaker and host at Sunnyside, a private retreat center in southern Michigan. He also devotes time to environmental stewardship of the surrounding lakes and woodlands, and to promoting Servant-Leadership. He can be reached via email at gasanfan@umich.edu.

CPSIA information can be obtained at www.ICGtesting.com
Printed in the USA
BVOW022058201112

306076BV00001B/25/P